SLOW PRODUCTIVITY

ALSO BY CAL NEWPORT

A World Without Email

Digital Minimalism

Deep Work

So Good They Can't Ignore You

How to Be a High School Superstar

How to Become a Straight-A Student

How to Win at College

SLOW PRODUCTIVITY

*The Lost Art of Accomplishment
Without Burnout*

Cal Newport

PORTFOLIO | PENGUIN

Portfolio / Penguin
An imprint of Penguin Random House LLC
penguinrandomhouse.com

Copyright © 2024 by Calvin C. Newport
Penguin Random House supports copyright. Copyright fuels creativity, encourages diverse voices, promotes free speech, and creates a vibrant culture. Thank you for buying an authorized edition of this book and for complying with copyright laws by not reproducing, scanning, or distributing any part of it in any form without permission. You are supporting writers and allowing Penguin Random House to continue to publish books for every reader.

Most Portfolio books are available at a discount when purchased in quantity for sales promotions or corporate use. Special editions, which include personalized covers, excerpts, and corporate imprints, can be created when purchased in large quantities. For more information, please call (212) 572-2232 or email specialmarkets@penguinrandomhouse.com. Your local bookstore can also assist with discounted bulk purchases using the Penguin Random House corporate Business-to-Business program. For assistance in locating a participating retailer, email B2B@penguinrandomhouse.com.

Library of Congress Cataloging-in-Publication Data
Names: Newport, Cal, author.
Title: Slow productivity : the lost art of accomplishment without burnout / Cal Newport.
Description: [New York] : Portfolio/Penguin, [2024] | Includes bibliographical references and index.
Identifiers: LCCN 2023033502 (print) | LCCN 2023033503 (ebook) | ISBN 9780593544853 (hardcover) | ISBN 9780593719435 (international edition) | ISBN 9780593544860 (ebook)
Subjects: LCSH: Labor productivity. | Humanism.
Classification: LCC HC79.L3 .N497 2024 (print) | LCC HC79.L3 (ebook) | DDC 331.11/8—dc23/eng/20231017
LC record available at https://lccn.loc.gov/2023033502
LC ebook record available at https://lccn.loc.gov/2023033503

Printed in the United States of America
4th Printing

Book design by Nicole LaRoche

To my family, for reminding me every day about the joys of slowing down.

CONTENTS

Introduction — 1

Part 1 | FOUNDATIONS

Chapter 1
The Rise and Fall of Pseudo-Productivity — 13

Chapter 2
A Slower Alternative — 31

Part 2 | PRINCIPLES

Chapter 3
Do Fewer Things — 47

Chapter 4
Work at a Natural Pace   *111*

Chapter 5
Obsess Over Quality   *165*

Conclusion   *213*

Acknowledgments   *221*
Notes   *223*
Index   *235*

SLOW PRODUCTIVITY

INTRODUCTION

In the summer of 1966, toward the end of his second year as a staff writer for *The New Yorker*, John McPhee found himself on his back on a picnic table under an ash tree in his backyard near Princeton, New Jersey. "I lay down on it for nearly two weeks, staring up into branches and leaves, fighting fear and panic," he recalls in his 2017 book, *Draft No. 4*. McPhee had already published five long-form articles for *The New Yorker* and, before that, had spent seven years as an associate editor for *Time*. He wasn't, in other words, new to magazine writing, but the article that immobilized him on his picnic table that summer was the most complicated he had yet attempted to write.

McPhee had previously written profiles, such as his first major piece for *The New Yorker*, "A Sense of Where You Are," which followed the Princeton University basketball star Bill Bradley. He had also written historical accounts: in the spring of 1966, he published a two-part article on oranges that traced the humble fruit's history all the way back to its first reference in 500 BCE in China. McPhee's current project, however, which tackled the impossibly broad topic of the Pine Barrens of southern New Jersey, was attempting to do much more. Instead of writing a focused profile, he had to weave the stories of multiple characters, including extensive re-creation of dialogue and visits to specific settings. Instead of summarizing the history of a single object, he had to dive into the geological, ecological, and even political backstory of an entire region.

McPhee spent eight months researching the topic in the lead-up to his picnic table paralysis, gathering what he later called "enough material to fill a silo." He had traveled from his Princeton home down to the Pine Barrens more times than he could easily remember, often bringing a sleeping bag to extend his stay. He had read all the relevant books and talked to all the relevant people. Now that he had to start writing, he felt overwhelmed. "To lack confidence at the outset seems rational to me," he explained. "It doesn't matter that something you've done before worked out well. Your last piece is never going to write your next one for you." So McPhee lay on his picnic table, looking up at the branches of that ash tree, trying to figure out how to make this lumbering mass of sources and stories work together. He stayed on that table for two weeks before a solution to his quandary finally arrived: Fred Brown.

Early in his research, McPhee had met Brown, a seventy-nine-year-old who lived in a "shanty" deep in the Pine Barrens. They had subsequently spent many days wandering the woods together. The revelation that jolted McPhee off his picnic table was that Brown seemed to be connected in some way to most of the topics that he wanted to cover in his article. He could introduce Brown early in the piece, and then structure the topics he wanted to explore as detours from the through line of his adventures with Brown.

Even after this moment of insight, it still took McPhee more than a year to finish writing his article, working in a modest rental office off Nassau Street in Princeton, located above an optometrist's shop and across the hall from a Swedish massage parlor. The finished piece would stretch to more than thirty thousand words and be divided into two parts, to appear in two consecutive issues of the magazine. It's a marvel of long-form reporting and one of the more beloved entries in McPhee's long bibliography. It couldn't have existed, however, without McPhee's willingness to put everything else on hold, and just lie on his back, gazing upward toward the sky, thinking hard about how to create something wonderful.

I came across this story of John McPhee's unhurried approach during the early days of the coronavirus pandemic, which was, to put it mildly, a complicated time for knowledge workers. As that anxious spring unfolded, a long-simmering unease with the demands of *productivity* among those who toil in offices and at computer screens for a living began to boil over under the strain of pandemic-related disruptions. As someone who often touched on productivity issues in my writing on technology and distraction, I experienced this intensifying backlash directly. "Productivity language is an impediment to me," one of my readers explained to me in an email. "The pleasure in thinking and doing things well is such a deep-wired human pleasure . . . and it feels (to me) diluted when it's linked to productivity." A commenter on my blog added, "The productivity terminology encodes not only getting things done, but doing them at all costs." The specific role of the pandemic as a driver of these sentiments was often evident in this feedback. As one insightful reader elaborated, "The fact that productivity = widgets produced is, if anything, clearer during this pandemic as parents fortunate enough to still have jobs are expected to produce similar amounts of work while caring for and educating kids." This energy surprised me. I love my audience, but *fired up* is not usually a term I used to describe them. Until now. Something was clearly changing.

As I soon discovered, this growing anti-productivity sentiment wasn't confined only to my readers. Between the spring of 2020 and the summer of 2021, a period spanning less than a year and a half, at least four major books were published that took direct aim at popular notions of productivity. These included Celeste Headlee's *Do Nothing*, Anne Helen Petersen's *Can't Even*, Devon Price's *Laziness Does Not Exist*, and Oliver Burkeman's delightfully sardonic *Four Thousand Weeks*. This exhaustion with work was also reflected in multiple waves of heavily reported social trends that crested one after another during the pandemic. First there was the so-called Great Resignation. Though this phenomenon encompassed retreats from labor force participation in many different economic sectors, among these many sub-narratives was a clear trend among knowledge workers to downgrade the demands of their careers. The Great Resignation was then followed by the rise of quiet quitting, in which a younger cohort of workers began to aggressively push back on their employers' demands for productivity.

"We are overworked and overstressed, constantly dissatisfied, and reaching for a bar that keeps rising higher and higher," writes Celeste Headlee in the introduction to *Do Nothing*. A few years earlier, this sentiment might have seemed provocative. By the time the pandemic peaked, however, she was preaching to the choir.

As I witnessed this fast-growing discontent, it became clear to me that something important was happening. Knowledge workers were exhausted—burned out from an increasingly relentless busyness. The pandemic didn't introduce this trend so much as push its worst excesses beyond the threshold of tolerability. More than a few knowledge workers, thrust suddenly into remote work, their kids screaming in the next room as they suffered through yet another Zoom meeting, began to wonder, "What are we really doing here?"

I began extensively covering knowledge worker discontent, as well as alternative constructions of professional meaning, on my long-standing newsletter, as well as on a new podcast I launched early in the pandemic. As the anti-productivity movement continued to pick up speed, I also began to cover the topic more frequently in my reporting for *The New Yorker*, where I'm on the contributor staff, ultimately leading, during the fall of 2021, to my taking on a twice-a-month column called Office Space that was dedicated to this subject.

The storylines I uncovered were complicated. People were overwhelmed, but the sources of this increasing exhaustion weren't obvious. Online discussion of these issues offered no shortage of varied, and sometimes contradictory, theories: Employers were relentlessly increasing the demands on their employees in an attempt to extract more value from their labor. No, it's actually an internalized culture valorizing busyness, driven by online productivity influencers, that's leading to our exhaustion. Or maybe what we're really seeing is the inevitable collapse of "last-stage capitalism." Fingers were pointed and frustrations vented; all the while, knowledge workers continued to descend into increasing unhappiness. The situation seemed dark, but as I continued my own research on this topic, a glimmer of optimism emerged, sparked by the very tale with which we opened this discussion.

When I first encountered the story of John McPhee's long days looking up at the leaves in his backyard, I received it nostalgically—a scene from a time long past, when those who made a living with their minds were actually given the time and space needed to craft impressive things. "Wouldn't it be nice to have a job like that where you didn't have to worry about being *productive*?" I thought. But eventually an insistent realization emerged. McPhee *was* productive. If you zoom out from what he was doing on that picnic table on those specific summer days in 1966 to instead consider his entire career, you'll find a writer who has, to date, published twenty-nine books, one of which won a Pulitzer Prize, and two of which were nominated for National Book Awards. He has also penned distinctive articles for *The New Yorker* for over five decades, and through his famed creative nonfiction course, which he has long taught at Princeton University, he has mentored many young writers who went on to enjoy their own distinctive careers, a list that includes Richard Preston, Eric Schlosser, Jennifer Weiner, and David Remnick. There's no reasonable definition of productivity that shouldn't also apply to John McPhee, and yet nothing about his work habits is frantic, busy, or overwhelming.

This initial insight developed into the core idea that this book will explore: perhaps knowledge workers' problem is not with productivity in a general sense, but instead with a specific faulty definition of this term that has taken hold in recent decades. The relentless overload that's wearing us down is generated by a belief that "good" work requires increasing busyness—faster responses to email and chats, more meetings, more tasks, more hours. But when we look closer at this premise, we fail to find a firm foundation. I came to believe that alternative approaches to productivity can be just as easily justified, including those in which overfilled task lists and constant activity are downgraded in importance, and something like John McPhee's languid intentionality is lauded. Indeed, it became clear that the habits and rituals of traditional knowledge workers like McPhee were more than just inspiring, but could, with sufficient care to account for the realities of twenty-first-century jobs, provide a rich source of ideas about how we might transform our modern understanding of professional accomplishment.

These revelations sparked new thinking about how we approach our work, eventually coalescing into a fully formed alternative to the assumptions driving our current exhaustion:

SLOW PRODUCTIVITY

A *philosophy for organizing knowledge work efforts in a sustainable and meaningful manner, based on the following three principles:*

1. Do fewer things.
2. Work at a natural pace.
3. Obsess over quality.

As you'll learn in the pages ahead, this philosophy rejects busyness, seeing overload as an obstacle to producing results that matter, not a badge of pride. It also posits that professional efforts should unfold at a more varied and humane pace, with hard periods counterbalanced by relaxation at many different timescales, and that a focus on impressive quality, not performative activity, should underpin everything. In the second part of this book, I'll detail the philosophy's core principles, providing both theoretical justification for why they're right and concrete advice on how to take action on them in your specific professional life, regardless of whether you run your own company or work under the close supervision of a boss.

My goal is not to simply offer tips about how to make your job somewhat less exhausting. Nor is it to merely shake my metaphorical fist on your behalf at the exploitative fiends indifferent to your stressed-out plight (though we'll certainly do some of that). I want to instead propose an *entirely new* way for you, your small business, or your large employer to think about what it means to get things done. I want to rescue knowledge work from its increasingly untenable freneticism and rebuild it into something more sustainable and humane, enabling you to create things you're proud of without requiring you to grind yourself down along the way. Not every office job, of course, will enjoy the ability to immediately embrace this more intentional rhythm, but as I'll detail, it's more widely applicable than you might at first guess. I want to prove to you, in other words, that accomplishment without burnout not only is possible, but should be the new standard.

Before we get ahead of ourselves, however, we must first understand how the knowledge sector stumbled into its current malfunctioning relationship with productivity in the first place, as it will be easier to reject the status quo once we truly understand the haphazardness of its formation. It's toward the pursuit of this goal, then, that we'll now start our journey.

Part 1

FOUNDATIONS

1 | THE RISE AND FALL OF PSEUDO-PRODUCTIVITY

In the summer of 1995, Leslie Moonves, the newly appointed head of entertainment for CBS, was wandering the halls of the network's vast Television City headquarters. He was not happy with what he saw: it was 3:30 p.m. on a Friday, and the office was three quarters empty. As the media journalist Bill Carter reports in *Desperate Networks*, his 2006 book about the television industry during this period, a frustrated Moonves sent a heated memo about the empty office to his employees. "Unless anybody hasn't noticed, we're in third place [in the ratings]," he wrote. "My guess is that at ABC and NBC they're still working at 3:30 on Friday. This will no longer be tolerated."

On first encounter, this vignette provides a stereotypical case study about the various ways the knowledge sector came to think about productivity during the twentieth century: "Work" is a vague thing that employees do in an office. More work creates better results than less. It's a manager's job to ensure *enough* work is getting done, because without this pressure, lazy employees will attempt to get away with the bare minimum. The most successful companies have the hardest workers.

But how did we develop these beliefs? We've heard them enough times to convince ourselves that they're probably true, but a closer look reveals a more complicated story. It doesn't take much probing to discover that in the knowledge work environment, when it comes to the basic goal of getting things done, we actually know much less than we're letting on . . .

What Does "Productivity" Mean?

As the full extent of our culture's growing weariness with "productivity" became increasingly apparent in recent years, I decided to survey my readers about the topic. My goal was to nuance my understanding of what was driving this shift. Ultimately, close to seven hundred people, almost all knowledge workers, participated in my informal study. My first substantive question was meant to be easy; a warm-up of sorts: "In your particular professional field, how would most people define 'productivity' or 'being productive'?" The responses I received to this initial query, however, surprised me. The issue was less what they said than what they didn't. By far the most common style of answer simply listed the *types* of things the respondent did in their job.

"Producing content and services for the benefit of our member organizations," replied an executive named Michael. "The ability to produce [sermons] while simultaneously caring for your flock via personal visits," said a pastor named Jason. A researcher named Marianna pointed to "attending meetings . . . running lab experiments . . . and producing peer-reviewed articles." An engineering director named George defined productivity to be "doing what you said you would do."

None of these answers included specific goals to meet, or performance measures that could differentiate between doing a job well versus badly. When quantity *was* mentioned, it tended to be in the general sense that more is always better. (Productivity is "working all the time," explained an exhausted postdoc named Soph.) As I read through more of my surveys, an unsettling revelation began to emerge: for all of our complaining about the term, knowledge workers have no agreed-upon definition of what "productivity" even means.

This vagueness extends beyond the self-reflection of individuals; it's also reflected in academic treatments of this topic. In 1999, the management theorist Peter Drucker published an influential paper titled "Knowledge-Worker Productivity: The Biggest Challenge." Early in the article, Drucker admits that "work on the productivity of the knowledge worker has barely begun." In an attempt to rectify this reality, he goes on to list six "major factors" that influence productivity in the knowledge sector, including clarity about tasks and a commitment to continuous learning and innovation. As in my survey responses, all of this is just him talking around the issue—identifying things that *might* support productive work in a general sense, not providing specific properties to measure, or processes to improve. A few years ago, I interviewed a distinguished Babson College management professor named Tom Davenport for an article. I was interested in Davenport because, earlier in his career, he was one of the few academics I could find who seriously attempted to study productivity in the knowledge sector, culminating in his 2005 book, *Thinking for a Living: How to Get Better Performance and Results from Knowledge Workers*. Davenport ultimately became frustrated with the difficulty of making meaningful progress on this topic and moved on to more rewarding areas. "In most cases, people don't measure the productivity of knowledge workers," he explained. "And when we do, we do it in really silly ways, like how many papers do academics produce, regardless of quality. We are still in the quite early stages." Davenport has written or edited twenty-five books. He told me that *Thinking for a Living* was the worst selling of them all.

It's hard to overemphasize how unusual it is that an economic sector as large as knowledge work lacks useful standard definitions of productivity. In most every other area of our economy, not only is productivity a well-defined concept, but it's often central to how work unfolds. Indeed, much of the astonishing economic growth fueling modernity can be attributed to a more systematic treatment of this fundamental idea. Early uses of the term can be traced back to agriculture, where its meaning is straightforward. For a farmer, the productivity of a given parcel of land can be measured by the amount of food the land produces. This ratio of output to input provides a compass of sorts that allows farmers to navigate the possible ways to cultivate their crops: systems that work better will produce measurably more bushels per acre. This use of a clear productivity metric to help improve clearly defined processes might sound obvious, but the introduction of this approach enabled explosive leaps forward in efficiency. In the seventeenth century, for example, it was exactly this type of metric-driven experimentation that led to the Norfolk four-course system of planting, which eliminated the need to leave fields fallow. This in turn made many farmers suddenly much more productive, helping to spur the British agricultural revolution.

As the Industrial Revolution began to emanate outward from Britain in the eighteenth century, early capitalists adapted similar notions of productivity from farm fields to their mills and factories. As with growing crops, the key idea was to measure the amount of output produced for a given amount of input and then experiment with different processes for improving this value. Farmers care about bushels per acre, while factory owners care about automobiles produced per paid hour of labor. Farmers might improve their metric by using a smarter crop rotation system, while factory owners might improve their metric by shifting production to a continuous-motion assembly line. In these examples, different types of things are being produced, but the force driving changes in methods is the same: productivity.

There was, of course, a well-known human cost to this emphasis on measurable improvement. Working on an assembly line is repetitive and boring, and the push for individuals to be more efficient in their every action creates conditions that promote injury and exhaustion. But the ability for productivity to generate astonishing economic growth in these sectors swept aside most such concerns. Assembly lines are dreary for workers, but when Henry Ford switched his factory in Highland Park, Michigan, to this method in 1913, the labor-hours required to produce a Model T dropped from 12.5 to around 1.5—a staggering improvement. By the end of the decade, half of the cars in the United States had been produced by the Ford Motor Company. These rewards were too powerful to resist. The story of economic growth in the modern Western world is in many ways a story about the triumph of productivity thinking.

But then the knowledge sector emerged as a major force in the mid-twentieth century, and this profitable dependence on crisp, quantitative, formal notions of productivity all but vanished. There was, as it turns out, a good reason for this abandonment: the old notions of productivity that worked so well in farming and manufacturing didn't seem to apply to this new style of cognitive work. One problem is the variability of effort. When the infamous efficiency consultant Frederick Winslow Taylor was hired to improve productivity at Bethlehem Steel in the early twentieth century, he could assume that each worker at the foundry was responsible for a single, clear task, like shoveling slag iron. This made it possible for him to precisely measure their output per unit of time and seek ways to improve this metric. In this particular example, Taylor ended up designing a better shovel for the foundry workers that carefully balanced the desire to move more iron per scoop while also avoiding unproductive overexertion. (In case you're wondering, he determined the optimal shovel load was twenty-one pounds.)

In knowledge work, by contrast, individuals are often wrangling complicated and constantly shifting workloads. You might be working on a client report at the same time that you're gathering testimonials for the company website and organizing an office party, all the while updating a conflict of interest statement that human resources just emailed you about. In this setting, there's no clear single output to track. And even if you do wade through this swamp of activity to identify the work that matters most—recall Davenport's example of counting a professor's academic publications—there's no easy way to control for the impact of unrelated obligations on each individual's ability to produce. I might have published more academic papers than you last year, but this might have been, in part, due to a time-consuming but important committee that you chaired. In this scenario, am I really a more productive employee?

A Henry Ford–style approach of improving systems instead of individuals also struggled to take hold in the knowledge work context. Manufacturing processes are precisely defined. At every stage of his development of the assembly line, Ford could detail exactly how Model Ts were produced in his factory. In the knowledge sector, by contrast, decisions about organizing and executing work are largely left up to individuals to figure out on their own. Companies might standardize the software that their employees use, but systems for assigning, managing, organizing, collaborating on, and ultimately executing tasks are typically left up to each individual. "The knowledge worker cannot be supervised closely or in detail," argued Peter Drucker in his influential 1967 book, *The Effective Executive*. "He can only be helped. But he must direct himself."

Knowledge work organizations took this recommendation seriously. The carefully engineered systems of factories were replaced with the "personal productivity" of offices, in which individuals deploy their own ad hoc and often ill-defined collection of tools and hacks to make sense of their jobs, with no one really knowing how anyone else is managing their work. In such a haphazard setting, there's no system to easily improve, no knowledge equivalent of the ten times productivity boost attributed to the assembly line. Drucker himself eventually grew to recognize the difficulties of pursuing productivity amid so much autonomy. "I think he did believe it was hard to improve . . . we let the inmates run the asylum, let them do the work as they wish," Tom Davenport told me, recalling conversations he had with Drucker in the 1990s.

These realities created a real problem for the emergent knowledge sector. Without concrete productivity metrics to measure and well-defined processes to improve, companies weren't clear how they should manage their employees. And as freelancers and small entrepreneurs in the sector became more prevalent, these individuals, responsible only for themselves, weren't sure how they should manage themselves. It was from this uncertainty that a simple alternative emerged: *using visible activity as a crude proxy for actual productivity*. If you can see me in my office—or, if I'm remote, see my email replies and chat messages arriving regularly—then, at the very least, you know I'm doing *something*. The more activity you see, the more you can assume that I'm contributing to the organization's bottom line. Similarly, the busier I am as a freelancer or entrepreneur, the more I can be assured I'm doing all I can to get after it.

As the twentieth century progressed, this visible-activity heuristic became the dominant way we began thinking about productivity in knowledge work. It's why we gather in office buildings using the same forty-hour workweeks originally developed for limiting the physical fatigue of factory labor, and why we feel guilty about ignoring our inboxes, or experience internalized pressure to volunteer or "perform busyness" when we see the boss is nearby. In the absence of more sophisticated measures of effectiveness, we also gravitate away from deeper efforts toward shallower, more concrete tasks that can be more easily checked off a to-do list. Long work sessions that don't immediately produce obvious contrails of effort become a source of anxiety—it's safer to chime in on email threads and "jump on" calls than to put your head down and create a bold new strategy. In her response to my reader survey, a social worker who identified herself only as N described the necessity of "not taking breaks, rushing, and hurrying all day," while a project manager named Doug explained that doing his job well reduced to "churning out lots of artifacts," whether they really mattered or not.

This switch from concrete productivity to this looser proxy heuristic is so important for our discussion to follow that we should give it a formal name and definition:

PSEUDO-PRODUCTIVITY

The use of visible activity as the primary means of approximating actual productive effort.

It's the vagueness of this philosophy that gave my readers so much trouble when I asked them to define "productivity." It's not a formal system that can be easily explained; it's more like a mood—a generic atmosphere of meaningful activity maintained through frenetic motion. Its flaws are also more subtle. For early knowledge workers, there were clear advantages to pseudo-productivity when compared with the concrete systems that organized industrial labor. Many people would rather pretend to be busy in an air-conditioned office than stamp sheet metal all day on a hot factory floor. As we'll see next, it really wasn't until the last couple of decades before an approach to work centered on pseudo-productivity derailed. But once it did, the damage was significant.

Why Are We So Exhausted?

The opening vignette about CBS is a classic demonstration of pseudo-productivity. Les Moonves needed better performance, so he turned the obvious knob: demanding his employees work longer hours. Another reason why I chose this specific story, however, was its timing. In the mid-1990s, when Moonves sent out his frustrated memo, the sustainability of pseudo-productivity as a means for organizing knowledge work had begun, seemingly all at once, to quietly but rapidly degrade.

The cause of this deterioration was the arrival during this decade of networked computers in the office. In a setting where activity provides a proxy for productivity, the introduction of tools like email (and, later, Slack) that make it possible to visibly signal your busyness with minimal effort inevitably led to more and more of the average knowledge worker's day being dedicated to talking *about* work, as fast and frantically as possible, through incessant electronic messaging. (One particularly damning analysis, conducted by the software company RescueTime, and based on log data from over ten thousand knowledge workers, revealed that the subjects they studied checked their inbox once every six minutes on average.) The subsequent arrival of portable computing and communication, in the form of laptops and smartphones, made this trend even worse, as the demand to demonstrate effort could now extend beyond the workday, following us home at night or to our kid's soccer field on the weekend. Computers and networks opened many new possibilities, but when combined with pseudo-productivity they ended up supercharging our sense of overload and distraction, pushing us onto a collision course with the burnout crisis that afflicts us today.

It's important to emphasize the magnitude of these current woes. A recent study conducted by McKinsey and Lean In, for example, which surveyed more than sixty-five thousand North

American employees, primarily from knowledge sector jobs, found a significant increase in those describing themselves as feeling burned out "often" or "almost always." A subsequent Gallup poll showed that American workers are now among some of the most stressed in the world. Jim Harter, Gallup's chief workplace scientist, noted that these stress measures rose alongside metrics that show an increase in employee efforts. "The intersection of work and life needs some work," he said.

We don't need data, however, to teach us what so many have already encountered in their own lives. The responses from my reader survey, for example, were filled with personal accounts of exhausting overload driven by new office technology. A strategic planner named Steve provided a good summary of this experience:

> It seems like the benefits of technology have created the ability to stack more into our day and onto our schedules than we have the capacity to handle while maintaining a level of quality which makes the things worth doing. . . . I think that's where the burnout really hurts—when you want to care about something but you're removed from the capacity to do the thing or do it properly and give it your passion and full attention and creativity because you're expected to do so many other things.

A professor named Sara noted a similar creep of this hyperactivity into the academic world, describing an onslaught of "a lot of back-and-forth emails, Slack, last-minute Zoom meetings, etc., which prevent me (and everyone in general, I feel) from actually having the time to do deep work, think, write, with high quality." A virtual assistant named Myra provided a unique perspective, as she could summarize what she noticed about the multiple knowledge workers that she served. "My clients are very busy, but are often so overwhelmed by everything they want or have to do, that it becomes difficult to recognize what the priorities are for them," she told me. "So they just try to work on a lot and hope they make progress that way."

There can be a sense of hopelessness embedded into these accounts. Concrete productivity metrics of the type that shaped the industrial sector will never properly fit in the more amorphous knowledge work setting. (Nor should we *want* them to fit, as this quantitative approach to labor ushers in its own stark inhumanities.) In the absence of this clarity, however, pseudo-productivity can seem like the only viable default option. And when this option is combined with low-friction communication tools and portable computing, the result is the ever-amplifying cycle of activity that pushes us, as Myra so aptly described, toward simply working a lot—cramming professional effort into every corner of our lives, hoping that this ceaseless action somehow adds up to something meaningful. Before we fully give in to this grim reality, however, it's worth reassessing pseudo-productivity's supposed inevitability. If we return one last time to our CBS story, and look beyond the simple arc of Les Moonves's hard-nosed managerial heroics, hints of a more nuanced way to think about getting things done in knowledge work begin to emerge.

Is a Better Approach Possible?

The uplifting conclusion to the CBS story is that the struggling network did end up reversing its fortunes, moving from last place to first in the ratings, where it remained for many years to follow. But what really explains this turnaround? A closer examination reveals that Les Moonves demanding his employees work longer hours likely had very little to do with it. A more convincing explanation can be found in the meandering efforts of a Las Vegas–based casino tram operator named Anthony Zuiker. In 1996, a twenty-six-year-old Zuiker, who was being paid eight dollars an hour to ferry tourists between the Mirage and Treasure Island hotels, found himself despairing. As a young adult, he had distinguished himself among his family and friends as someone with a natural talent for attention-catching writing. He was now at a loss to figure out how to deliver on these skills. "In [Zuiker's] darkest moments," writes Bill Carter in *Desperate Networks*, "he found himself asking God why he had been given these unusual talents if he was never going to get a chance to use them."

The shift in Zuiker's fortunes began with an original monologue he wrote for an actor friend to use in his auditions. A Hollywood agent who heard the monologue tracked down Zuiker and asked if he wanted to try to write a screenplay. Zuiker bought a Syd Field book about screenwriting and crafted a spec script called *The Runner*, which told the story of a gambling addict who becomes a runner for a mobster. The script sold for a modest amount, but this was enough to put Zuiker on the radar of a new division of director Jerry Bruckheimer's production company that was looking to get more involved in television. They invited Zuiker to pitch them ideas. Inspired by a Discovery Channel reality show he enjoyed, *The New Detectives: Case Studies in Forensic Science*, Zuiker came up with a premise for a procedural police show, similar to *Law & Order*, in which high-tech tools would be used to solve crimes.

Bruckheimer's company was interested and requested a script for a pilot. To research the plot, Zuiker began spending time with the Las Vegas police department. In one memorable encounter, the crime investigation team asked him to comb a bedroom carpet in search of clues. As Zuiker bent down with his comb, he saw the drug-addled eyes of the suspect, who was hiding under the bed. She swiped at Zuiker with her nails before the officers on the scene subdued her. "Oh, this is for sure a show," Zuiker quipped. Eventually, he was ready to present his idea to a network. "Zuiker wove his pitch magic for a group of executives from the ABC drama department," writes Carter, "jumping around the room, leaping on furniture, and bringing his characters to vivid life." Despite his energy, ABC still passed.

Now fully invested in his vision, Zuiker reacted to this failure by forming his own production company, Dare to Pass, dedicated to the singular goal of bringing his crime investigation show to life. After attracting the interest of a CBS executive named Nina Tassler, Zuiker sweated through another three rewrites of the pilot script in an effort to move it closer to something airable. Tassler brought this improved script to Moonves, who didn't quite get it and tabled the project. Zuiker and Tassler kept working. They attached a well-known television director named Billy Peterson, who wrote a letter to Moonves making a passionate case for Zuiker's show. Moonves read the letter and was finally convinced: CBS would finance a pilot.

Even then, however, the project struggled. The pilot was finished late, and when it was previewed by CBS executives over lunch, it was clear it still wasn't working. Moonves in particular felt the story was hard to follow. "You guys have to dig deep and redo this thing," he said. The team rushed to reedit the episode. Time was short: for the show to make it on the air in the fall, it had to be ready to showcase to advertisers at an up-front event scheduled only a few months later. The final decision on the show was made at the absolute last minute, at a scheduling meeting held right before the deadline for CBS to announce its fall slate of programs. In the end, Moonves had to choose between Zuiker's show and a Tony Danza comedy called *Homewood P.I.* for Friday evenings—the last available open slot. He went with his gut and chose Zuiker. This decision proved momentous. Zuiker's project, which was eventually named *CSI*, was an immediate hit when it first aired a few months later in the fall of 2000. When combined with CBS's other breakout success of that season, *Survivor*, the ratings boost was enough to vault CBS into first place.

The details of CBS's turnaround provide a useful contrast between differing conceptions of productivity. Moonves tried to save his network by pushing his employees to work more. What ended up mattering, however, was instead the obsessive efforts of an eccentric creative talent who spent over three years nurturing a vision, coming at it again and again in an attempt to create something special.* Anthony Zuiker's efforts were far more varied in their type and intensity than what Moonves was demanding of his employees. Zuiker didn't show up at an office every day or dutifully make his presence known in endless meetings. There were long stretches during the development of *CSI* in which Zuiker's visible activity would have been minimal, balanced by other stretches that were more intense. But when you zoom out to the scale of years, his productivity is unmistakable—who cares, for example, if he rested for a month in 1999, when he ultimately saved the network by 2000?

Like John McPhee waiting on the picnic table for insight on his article structure, Zuiker's efforts point toward a definition of meaningful and valuable work that doesn't require a frenetic busyness. Its magic instead becomes apparent at longer timescales, emanating from a pace that seems, in comparison with the relentless demands of high-tech pseudo-productivity, to be, for lack of a better word, almost *slow*.

---

* It should be noted, of course, that the eventual realization of Zuiker's creative efforts also required the bold support of CBS executive Nina Tassler. This massive contribution from Tassler had little to do with working late or demonstrating busyness. It was instead much more about the application of creative instincts forged through long experience. These are the types of actions that ultimately make the difference in breakout success, not dramatic demonstrations of work ethic.

2 | A SLOWER ALTERNATIVE

In 1986, McDonald's announced a plan to open a massive new restaurant, with seating for over 450 people, at the Piazza di Spagna in Rome, near the base of the Spanish Steps. Many Italians weren't pleased. City council members tried to block the opening, while the fashion designer Valentino, who maintained a studio in the area, argued that the smell of hamburgers would sully his couture outfits. "What disturbs us most is the Americanization of our life," decried the film director Luciano De Crescenzo. The mayor put together a special garbage squad to hunt down the errant hamburger wrappers that he assumed would soon fill the streets.

It was amid this unrest that a seasoned activist and journalist named Carlo Petrini launched a new movement that he called Slow Food. A corresponding manifesto defined its goals:

> Against those—or, rather, the vast majority—who confuse efficiency with frenzy, we propose the vaccine of an adequate

portion of sensual gourmandise pleasures, to be taken with slow and prolonged enjoyment.

Appropriately, we will start in the kitchen, with Slow Food. To escape the tediousness of "fast-food," let us rediscover the rich varieties and aromas of local cuisines.

Across Italy, other local Slow Food chapters began to emerge. The group promoted slow meals, eaten communally, made from local and seasonal ingredients. After a while, they took on related goals, such as the introduction of regional food curricula into local grammar schools, and efforts to preserve traditional foods, like the delicious Vesuvian apricot, native to the Campania region in southern Italy. In 1996, the movement organized the first Salone del Gusto in Turin to support local food traditions and artisans. Held biannually, the event now attracts over 200,000 visitors who can sample from over 1,500 stalls. Today, there are Slow Food chapters in 160 countries.

On the surface, Slow Food might seem like a niche movement—a nostalgia-tinged gathering of foodies who obsess over the culinary possibilities of Italian apricots. Until recently, that's how I would have thought of it, if I had occasion to think about it at all. As I began grappling with the issues surrounding knowledge work and pseudo-productivity, however, Carlo Petrini's bid for deliberativeness at the table entered my thinking in a surprisingly major way.

The Slowness Revolution

I first stumbled into the world of Slow Food because of my attraction to the word *slow*, which seemed to capture everything that pseudo-productivity was not. I knew the basics of the movement's story—McDonald's, Rome, long dinners—and thought it might provide a useful analogy when talking about alternatives to the accelerated pace of work. As I read more about Petrini, however, I discovered that Slow Food is about more than meals, it's an instantiation of two deep, innovative ideas that can be applied to many different attempts to build a reform movement in response to the excesses of modernity.

The first such idea is the power of appealing alternatives. As Michael Pollan summarizes in an insightful 2003 article about Slow Food, by the 1980s Carlo Petrini had become "dismayed by the hangdog dourness of his comrades on the left." There's a personal satisfaction in grimly pointing out the flaws in a system, but sustainable change, Petrini came to believe, requires providing people with an enjoyable and life-affirming alternative. Petrini didn't simply write a sharply worded op-ed about the corruptive forces of McDonald's, he instead promoted an appealing new relationship with food that would make fast food seem self-evidently vulgar. "Those who suffer for others do more damage to humanity than those who enjoy themselves," Petrini explained.

The second idea intertwined with Slow Food is the power of pulling from time-tested cultural innovations. There's a temptation in activism to propose radically *new* ideas, as this preserves the utopian possibility of a pristine solution. Petrini recognized, however, that when it came to presenting an appealing alternative to fast food, he would be wise to draw from *traditional* food cultures that had developed through trial-and-error experimentation over many generations. Slow Food doesn't just support longer meals, it promotes a style of communal dining that had been common in Italian villages for centuries. It doesn't just support fresher ingredients, it recommended dishes that your great-great-grandmother might have served. Traditions that survived the gauntlet of cultural evolution, he believed, are more likely to catch on.

In his 2003 article, Pollan admits that he was at first skeptical of this nostalgic aspect of the movement, writing early in his essay, "Slow Foodies were antiquarian connoisseurs, I figured, with about as much to contribute to the debate over the food system as a colloquium of buggy whip fanciers might have to add to the debate over SUVs." As he learned more about Petrini's innovative activism, however, his attitude changed. Slow Food wasn't looking backward to escape the present, but instead to find ideas to help reshape the future. Pollan goes on to recant his initial skepticism and admits that the movement had "a serious contribution to make to the debate over environmentalism and globalism."

Once isolated, Petrini's two big ideas for developing reform movements—focus on alternatives to what's wrong and draw these solutions from time-tested traditions—are obviously not restricted to food in any fundamental sense. They can apply to any setting in which a haphazard modernism is conflicting with the human experience. This claim is validated by the many new *slow* movements that arose in the wake of Slow Food's original success, targeting other aspects of our culture that were suffering from an unthinking haste.

As the journalist Carl Honoré documents in his 2004 book, *In Praise of Slowness*, these second-wave movements include Slow Cities, which also started in Italy (where it's called Cittaslow), and focuses on making cities more pedestrian-centric, supportive of local business, and, in a general sense, more neighborly. They also include Slow Medicine, which promotes the holistic care of people as opposed to focusing only on disease, and Slow Schooling, which attempts to free elementary school students from the pressures of high-stakes testing and competitive tracking. More recently, the Slow Media movement has emerged to promote more sustainable and higher-quality alternatives to digital clickbait, and the term Slow Cinema is increasingly used to describe realistic, largely non-narrative movies that reward extended attention with deeper insight into the human condition. "The slow movement was first seen as an idea for a few people who liked to eat and drink well," explained the mayor of Petrini's hometown of Bra. "But now it has become a much broader cultural discussion about the benefits of doing things in a more human, less frenetic manner."

Slow Food. Slow Cities. Slow Medicine. Slow Schooling. Slow Media. Slow Cinema. All movements built on the radical but effective strategy of offering people a slower, more sustainable alternative to modern busyness that draws from time-tested wisdom. As I learned more about these ideas in my reporting on knowledge work, a natural follow-up thought emerged: maybe when it comes to combating the inhumanity of our current moment of professional overload, what we really need—more so than righteous disdain or brash new policy—is a slower conception of what it even means to be productive in the first place.

In Search of a Better Alternative

One of the intriguing developments of the immediate post-pandemic period is the opportunity it presents for major overhauls of how knowledge work operates. The disruptive retreat to virtual meetings and home offices in the spring of 2020 shook this sector out of its business-as-usual complacency. As the distraction of the health emergency dissipated, more than a few former cubicle dwellers were left wondering what other major changes might be possible.

We see this new attitude reflected in the wrangling that emerged between employees and bosses over plans to return to office buildings. In the spring of 2022, when Apple CEO Tim Cook announced that employees would be required to work in person at the company's Cupertino headquarters at least some days each week, the protest in response was swift and intense. "Stop treating us like school kids who need to be told when to be where and what homework to do," demanded an open letter addressed to Cook by an employee group called AppleTogether. In the months that followed, Cook repeatedly delayed the office return plan in response to this resistance. A full year after Cook's original announcement, as I'm writing this chapter, the battle continues, with Cook now openly threatening to punish employees who still refuse to return. "Those frustrated Apple employees aren't just arguing about their commutes," I wrote in a

New Yorker article reporting on this fight. "They're at the vanguard of a movement that's leveraging the disruptions of the pandemic to question so many more of the arbitrary assumptions that have come to define the modern workplace."

This new focus on major transformations is also reflected in rising interest in the four-day workweek. In February 2023, the UK released the results of a large-scale pilot study that followed more than sixty companies that experimented with a reduced schedule. As the BBC reported, the results were "overwhelming positive," with more than 90 percent of the participating companies claiming they would keep going with the experimental setup, at least for now. Here in America, California congressman Mark Takano proposed legislation that would officially reduce the standard workweek, as established by the Fair Labor Standards Act, from forty to thirty-two hours. Though his bill didn't gain traction, companies such as Lowe's and Kickstarter are already experimenting with these shorter schedules on their own.

This sudden interest in workplace experimentation is both welcome and needed, as much about how we work in the knowledge sector today is ossified into tradition and conventions, some of which are arbitrary and some of which are borrowed from different, older types of work. The proposals making waves at the moment, however, feel somehow insufficient on their own. Moves to maintain telecommuting or reduce the workweek help blunt some of the worst side effects of pseudo-productivity but do little to address the root problem itself. These ideas are the work equivalent of responding to the growth of fast-food culture by demanding McDonald's make its meals somewhat more nutritious—it would help tame some of the health impacts of this food, but not challenge the culture that makes hasty eating necessary in the first place.

As Carlo Petrini taught us, a more sustainable response to the burnout crisis facing knowledge work would be to offer an appealing alternative. This would require moving beyond attempts to simply constrain pseudo-productivity to instead propose a brand-new vision of what productivity can mean. The challenge, of course, is figuring out the details of such an alternative. This is where Petrini's second big idea becomes relevant: draw from time-tested ideas. If we informally think of knowledge work as people sitting in office buildings typing into computers, we might despair about finding traditional wisdom relevant to such a decidedly modern activity. To make progress with Petrini's slow framework, let's instead consider the following, more expansive formulation:

KNOWLEDGE WORK (GENERAL DEFINITION)

The economic activity in which knowledge is transformed into an artifact with market value through the application of cognitive effort.

This definition still captures standard office-bound employees, such as computer programmers, marketers, accountants, executives, and so on. But it now also captures many other cognitive professions that have been around longer than the Age of Cubicles. By this definition, for example, writers are knowledge workers, as are philosophers, scientists, musicians, playwrights, and artists. These more traditional cognitive professions, of course, are often more rarefied than standard office jobs—professional musicians, or renaissance scientists supported by patrons, have way more flexibility and options in designing their work life than, say, an HR coordinator. It's easy to therefore reject these case studies with a dismissive nod to privilege. (I can see the tweet now: "It must be nice to have Lorenzo de' Medici paying your bills!") Though satisfying, this isn't a useful response, given our broader goals. It's exactly these rarefied freedoms that make traditional knowledge workers interesting to our project, as it provided them the space and time needed to experiment and figure out what works best when it comes to sustainably creating valuable things using the human brain. *Of course*, most of us cannot directly replicate the specific details of, say, John McPhee's workday. What we're looking for, however, is not a blueprint to follow exactly, but general ideas that we can export from this exotic territory to the more pragmatic constraints of standard twenty-first-century knowledge sector jobs. I might not be able to spend two full weeks lying on a picnic table in my backyard, but there's a key insight lurking in that story about the value of slowing down to prepare to tackle a hard project. If we can get over our frustration that these traditional knowledge workers enjoyed privileges that we don't have access to, we might find in their experience the foundations for a conception of productivity that makes our harder jobs more manageable.

Once you start looking for these McPhee-style slower professional habits among traditional knowledge workers, it's easy to find a variety of examples. Consider Isaac Newton working through the details of calculus in the countryside north of Cambridge University, or a sculptor named Anna Rubincam, who documented in a beautifully edited video posted online how she plies her craft in a utilitarian studio in South London, the doors thrown open to a quiet tree-lined patio beyond. (The reader who sent me this clip titled her message "Epitome of deep work." I agreed.) A particularly entertaining diversion is uncovering the eccentric spaces where famous novelists would hide away to write. As I'll elaborate later, Peter Benchley, the author of *Jaws*, composed his classic thriller in the back room of a furnace repair shop, and Maya Angelou preferred scrawling on legal pads while propped up on her elbows on generic hotel room beds.

By early 2022, I was finally ready to pull together all my thoughts on how to apply Carlo Petrini's slow movement framework to the problems generated by pseudo-productivity. It was in an article that I published around that time that I gave my emerging philosophy a name—a natural title, given the sources of my inspiration, that I've used ever since: *slow productivity*.

A New Philosophy

The second part of this book is dedicated to elaborating a philosophy of slow productivity—an alternative framework knowledge workers can use to organize and execute tasks that sidesteps the hurry and ever-expanding workloads generated by pseudo-productivity. My goal is to offer a more humane and sustainable way to integrate professional efforts into a life well lived. To embrace slow productivity, in other words, is to reorient your work to be a source of meaning instead of overwhelm, while still maintaining the ability to produce valuable output.

To better understand what this entails, let's return to the formal definition first presented in the introduction:

SLOW PRODUCTIVITY

A philosophy for organizing knowledge work efforts in a sustainable and meaningful manner, based on the following three principles:

1. *Do fewer things.*
2. *Work at a natural pace.*
3. *Obsess over quality.*

At the core of this philosophy are three central principles. Accordingly, part 2 of this book is divided into three long chapters, one for each of these ideas. I start these chapters by explaining the corresponding recommendation, providing justification for why it's critical to the goal of achieving a more sustainable work life. These justifications are then followed by a series of *propositions* that detail specific ideas for implementing the principle within the messy realities of a standard knowledge work job. It's here that you'll find concrete advice and strategies that you can adapt as needed to your particular professional circumstance. Each chapter also includes an *interlude*, which provides self-reflective commentary and critique on the ideas being developed. I included these sections to underscore the reality that these ideas are new and complicated, and not everyone will receive them the same way. My hope is that you'll bring your own unique experiences to these propositions, allowing you to cultivate your own unique collection of insights and conclusions in response.

True to Carlo Petrini's vision, part 2 is rich in stories and examples drawn from the lives of traditional knowledge workers in a variety of different fields and time periods. You'll learn, for example, about Jane Austen, Ben Franklin, and Galileo, in addition to somewhat more modern figures such as Georgia O'Keeffe, Lin-Manuel Miranda, and Mary Oliver. I'll use these stories as the source of the ideas that I'll then polish into more pragmatic advice, adapted to the realities of modern jobs. But it's worth noting that the general mindset and mood conveyed in these tales are also of stand-alone value. Following Petrini's lead, I'm convinced that one of the best ways to truly introduce you to the "lost art of accomplishment without burnout" is to immerse you in the world of those who successfully built their lives around this goal.

Before diving into these specifics, however, I want to reassure you that slow productivity doesn't ask that you extinguish ambition. Humans derive great satisfaction from being good at what they do and producing useful things. This philosophy can be understood as providing a more sustainable path toward these achievements. Few people know, for example, how long it actually took Isaac Newton to develop all the ideas contained in his masterwork, the *Principia* (over twenty years). They just know that his book, once published, changed science forever. The value of his ideas lives on, while the lazy pace at which they were produced was soon forgotten. Slow productivity supports legacy-building accomplishments but allows them to unfold at a more human speed.

Though this book is about knowledge work productivity in general, it targets in particular anyone who has a reasonable degree of autonomy in their job. This obviously include freelancers, solopreneurs, and those who run small businesses. Pseudo-productivity's presence in these particular settings is not due to a boss's demands but is instead largely self-imposed, which opens up vast potential for individual experimentation. My imagined audience, however, also includes those who might work for larger employers but still enjoy significant freedom in how they go about their work. As a professor, for example, I fall into this latter definition, as would, say, a product designer who is expected to effectively disappear until she's ready to bring a new idea back to the team, or a fully remote worker whose output is tracked only at a rough granularity.

Those who instead work in an office environment under close supervision might have a harder time fully instituting the strategies I suggest. As will those whose efforts are highly structured, such as a doctor moving through an inflexible patient schedule, or a first-year law associate evaluated primarily on their accumulation of billable hours. This is not to say that slow productivity cannot one day reform these corners of knowledge work as well (see my discussion in the conclusion of this book about my broader vision for the future of this movement), but every revolution needs a starting point, and for something as momentous as rethinking the very notion of productivity itself, it makes sense to focus at first on those for whom self-experimentation is possible.

It's with these goals and caveats in mind that we now proceed . . .

Part 2

PRINCIPLES

3 DO FEWER THINGS

The First Principle of Slow Productivity

In late October 1811, an advertisement in a London newspaper promoted "a new novel by a lady." The author's name was not given, but in a subsequent advertisement, appearing the next month, she was more specifically identified as "Lady A." The book was *Sense and Sensibility*, and the pseudonymous author, of course, was Jane Austen, making her publishing debut. Austen had spent more than a decade working on a collection of manuscripts that she was now, seemingly all at once, polishing into impressive final forms. *Sense and Sensibility* initiated a remarkable five-year run of publishing, arguably unmatched in the history of modern literature, that saw Austen soon after also release *Pride and Prejudice*, *Mansfield Park*, and then finally, in 1815, *Emma*. Two years later, she died, all of only forty-one years old.

A popular explanation for Austen's productivity is that she mastered the art of writing secretly, scribbling prose in bursts between the many distracting obligations of her social standing. The source of this idea was Austen's nephew James, who in 1869, more than fifty years after Austen's death, published a gauzy Victorian biography of his aunt that helped expose her works to a broader audience. In chapter 6 of this memoir, James provides the following memorable description:

> How she was able to effect all this is surprising, for she had no separate study to retire to, and most of the work must have been done in the general sitting-room, subject to all kinds of casual interruptions. She was careful that her occupation should not be suspected by servants, or visitors, or any persons beyond her own family party. She wrote upon small sheets of paper which could easily be put away, or covered with a piece of blotting paper. There was, between the front door and the offices, a swing door which creaked when it was opened; but she objected to having this little inconvenience remedied, because it gave her notice when anyone was coming.

This story of the aspiring but frustrated gentlewoman, surreptitiously plying her craft, could have come straight out of one of Austen's novels. Not surprisingly, given this pleasing symmetry, this myth stuck. It's retold in modern accounts, such as Mason Currey's delightful 2013 book, *Daily Rituals*, as well as in older attempts to grapple with Austen's world. "Yet Jane Austen was glad that a hinge creaked, so that she might hide her manuscript before anyone came in," repeats Virginia Woolf in 1929 in *A Room of One's Own*.

This story can serve multiple purposes. Woolf, for example, uses it as part of an argument about gender roles and intellectual autonomy. Less sophisticated accounts enshrine it as a devotional about not giving up on your dreams. But when we turn our focus to the topic of productivity, James's portrayal of his aunt becomes suddenly disquieting. It seems to endorse a model of production in which better results require you to squeeze ever more work into your schedule. The obstacle standing between you and your own *Sense and Sensibility*, it implies, is a willingness to do more. Austen used small gaps between interminable social visits to write on scraps of paper in her sitting room, so why can't you wake up at 5:00 a.m. or make better use of your lunch hour?

A closer look at Austen's life, however, soon reveals issues with her nephew's tales of secret writing. Modern biographies, drawing more extensively from primary source material, reveal that the real Jane Austen was not an exemplar of a grind-it-out busyness, but instead a powerful case study of something quite different: a slower approach to productivity.

Jane Austen grew up in late eighteenth-century England, in the rural Hampshire village of Steventon, on what was essentially a small working farm. There were cows to milk and poultry to tend. Her family baked bread and brewed their own beer. In the summer the kids were given hay rakes and boiled jams and jellies. In the fall, they helped bring in the harvest. While Austen was still a young girl, her father, the rector for their parish, turned the parsonage in which they lived into an impromptu boys' school, adding the demands of the care and feeding of a half dozen stampeding boys to the list of daily chores.

This is not to say that the Austen family was strictly working class. As Claire Tomalin explains in her 1997 biography, *Jane Austen: A Life*, they inhabited a social world of "pseudo-gentry," made up of "families who aspired to live by the values of the gentry without owning land or inherited wealth of any significance." But it's clear that Austen did not grow up like a character in one of her books, spending her days in a well-appointed sitting room, taking visitors while servants prepared lavish meals. She had work to do. Though Austen was a voracious reader and, encouraged by her father, began dabbling in writing at a young age, she was much too busy with the daily work of running her family's house, farm, and school to seriously explore the craft.

This all changed in the summer of 1796 when Austen's father decided to close the boys' school run out of their house. "[This led to the] easing of all the work involved in the planning and preparation of meals, laundry, cleaning and bed making," writes Tomalin. And with her obligations suddenly dramatically reduced, Austen entered a period of "phenomenal" productivity. Working at an upstairs desk, reading drafts of her work to her family during the evening, she produced early versions of what would eventually become three major novels. As Tomalin emphasizes, it was Austen's ability to "abstract herself from the daily life going on around her" that allowed her to find her literary voice.

In 1800, this period of greatly reduced responsibilities abruptly ended when Austen's parents decided, seemingly out of nowhere, to shut down the house in Steventon and move to the resort town of Bath. For the next decade, Austen found herself constantly on the move, navigating the transition from one new household to another, taking on more duties as she coped with the sickness and eventual death of her father. Robbed of the ability to establish the "rhythm of work," as Tomalin puts it, Austen stopped writing.

The world would have been denied Austen's brilliance if not for a fateful decision made in 1809 that swung the conditions for productivity dramatically back in Austen's favor. Exhausted from the tumultuous past decade, Austen along with her mother, her sister, Cassandra, and their family friend Martha Lloyd settled into a modest cottage, positioned at the crossroads of the sleepy town of Chawton. The house was part of a large estate, owned by Austen's brother Edward, who had inherited the land from distant relatives of the Austen family who never had kids of their own and had years earlier named Edward their legal heir.

Critically for Austen's work, her family, wrung out from the complications and trials of the preceding years, embraced a much-needed respite by deciding to largely absent themselves from the social scene in Chawton. This was not a decision made lightly. The fact that Austen's brother essentially owned the town, and lived in an impressive estate just a few hundred yards down the road, meant that opportunities for active social striving were likely abundant. But the Austen party wasn't interested. "There were no dances and few dinners," writes Tomalin, "and they remained largely withdrawn into their private activities."

Austen's mother, now in her seventies, took to working in the garden of their cottage, wearing the frock of a day laborer, to the amusement of other town residents. Equally important, a tacit agreement was formed that would free the youngest Austen daughter from most of the remaining household labor. She prepared the morning breakfast for the family but, beyond this duty, was free to write. "In this way she was privileged with a general exemption from domestic chores when Cass and Martha were at home," explains Tomalin.

Hidden from the world at Chawton cottage, suddenly, almost miraculously free of most responsibilities both domestic and social, Austen, for the first time in over a decade, had gained real and meaningful space to think and work creatively. It's here, working at a modest writing desk by a window overlooking the road, that she finally finishes the manuscripts for *Sense and Sensibility* and *Pride and Prejudice* before moving on to compose *Mansfield Park* and *Emma*.

Austen's nephew may have popularized the story of an overscheduled Austen, prim and proper in her sitting room, working in frenzied bursts between incessant distractions, but the reality of her remarkable years at Chawton is clearly quite different.* Far

---

* An interesting parallel to the myth of Jane Austen's sitting room productivity can be found in the example of J. R. R. Tolkien. According to Tolkien biographer Raymond Edwards, it was commonly believed by some that Tolkien wrote the first stories for his *Book of Lost Tales*, his first attempts toward the mythologies that would develop into his famed fantasies, while under fire in the hellish trenches of the World War I battalion to which he was stationed. As Edwards notes, Tolkien himself later "pointed out the sheer impracticality of connected literary work under those conditions," calling this claim a "spoof." The reality is that Tolkien didn't start writing his *Lost Tales* until he was convalescing from trench fever in a British hospital, a circumstance, not unlike Austen's Chawton cottage, in which he found himself suddenly granted expansive free time. Raymond Edwards, *Tolkien* (Ramsbury, UK: The Crowood Press, 2022), 96.

from glamorizing a surreptitious, disciplined busyness, Austen's story, when told properly, seems to promote the opposite of this approach. Austen was *not* able to produce creatively during the crowded periods of her life. It was only when, through circumstance and contrivance, her obligations were greatly reduced that Austen was able, finally, to complete her best work.

This lesson, that doing less can enable better results, defies our contemporary bias toward activity, based on the belief that doing more keeps our options open and generates more opportunities for reward. But recall that *busy* Jane Austen was neither happy nor producing memorable work, while *unburdened* Jane Austen, writing contently at quiet Chawton cottage, transformed English literature.

Indeed, simplifying is so important to our emerging philosophy that I'll enshrine it here as the official first principle of slow productivity:

PRINCIPLE #1: DO FEWER THINGS

Strive to reduce your obligations to the point where you can easily imagine accomplishing them with time to spare. Leverage this reduced load to more fully embrace and advance the small number of projects that matter most.

The request made here, of course, is easier explained than actually implemented. In the context of your professional life, busyness likely seems unavoidable. Clients demand attention, and managers drown you in requests. Even if you're a solopreneur in full control of your days, the need for income might undermine your intention to reduce your workload. Jane Austen's long writing sessions at her desk in Chawton cottage can seem a fantastic mirage for the knowledge worker facing an endlessly full inbox.

My goal in this chapter is to persuade you not to give up on this aspirational vision of engineered simplicity. It *is* possible in most modern work settings, if you're willing to be creative—and perhaps, at times, even radical—in how you think about selecting and organizing your work. In the pages ahead, I'll detail my case for why a commitment to simplicity can be just as beneficial (and achievable) in modern knowledge work as it was for Austen's Victorian-era fiction writing, and then detail some concrete tactics for implementing this first principle of slow productivity.

From Chawton Cottage to the Cubicle; or, Why Knowledge Workers Should Do Fewer Things

In the spring of 2021, a program manager at HSBC named Jonathan Frostick, working remotely from his home office, suffered a heart attack. We know this because he subsequently posted a picture of himself in his hospital bed on LinkedIn, annotated with a list of six resolutions about how he would change his life if he survived. The post went viral, generating close to three hundred thousand comments online and attracting coverage from international media.

The Frostick incident caught my attention because of what he chose as his very first resolution among the six he listed: "I'm not spending all day on Zoom anymore." As Frostick later elaborated in a *Bloomberg* interview, during the first year of the pandemic, he dedicated an increasing amount of time to video calls. As a result, his workdays began to stretch out. "Whereas before I would finish sensibly anywhere between five and half past six, I'd be finding myself there on a Friday at 8 o'clock at night exhausted, thinking I need to prep up something for Monday and I haven't got time," he said. "I started then to actually work weekends." Frostick wasn't alone in feeling overwhelmed by his schedule during this period. A work trends report published by Microsoft revealed that time spent in meetings had increased by a factor of 2.5 during the first year of the pandemic, while the quantity of instant message chats and emails received also exploded. As the report summarizes, "The digital intensity of workers' days has increased substantially."

Most knowledge workers, of course, don't need statistics to convince them of a trend that they experienced directly. As 2020 gave way to 2021, I began to regularly hear from readers complaining that they were losing more or less their entire day to back-to-back-to-back virtual meetings, with nearly every moment of downtime in between filled with hyperactive Slack chatter. The reports became so dire that I took to referring to this period as the Zoom Apocalypse. Which is all to say, it's not surprising that Jonathan

Frostick had a heart attack and that his primary resolution on recovering was to escape this video conference hell. The important question for our purposes, however, is why this all happened in the first place.

In knowledge work, when you agree to a new commitment, be it a minor task or a large project, it brings with it a certain amount of ongoing administrative overhead: back-and-forth email threads needed to gather information, for example, or meetings scheduled to synchronize with your collaborators. This *overhead tax* activates as soon as you take on a new responsibility. As your to-do list grows, so does the total amount of overhead tax you're paying. Because the number of hours in the day is fixed, these administrative chores will take more and more time away from your core work, slowing down the rate at which these objectives are accomplished.

At moderate workloads, this effect might be frustrating: a general sense that completing your work is taking longer than it should. As your workload increases, however, the overhead tax you're paying will eventually pass a tipping point, beyond which logistical efforts will devour so much of your schedule that you cannot complete old tasks fast enough to keep up with the new. This feedback loop can quickly spiral out of control, pushing your workload higher and higher until you find yourself losing your entire day to overhead activities: meeting after meeting conducted against a background hum of unceasing email and chat. Eventually the only solution becomes to push actual work into ad hoc sessions added after hours—in the evenings and early mornings, or over the weekend—in a desperate attempt to avoid a full collapse of all useful output. You're as busy as you've ever been, and yet hardly get anything done.

It's exactly this dynamic that explains the Zoom Apocalypse. To see why, let's take a closer look at what changed for knowledge workers like Jonathan Frostick when the pandemic arrived. This health emergency affected different economic sectors in different ways. In knowledge work, the obvious disruption was the shift to telecommuting, which created a sudden influx of new tasks centered on adjusting our jobs to function outside an office. As a college professor, for example, I remember scrambling during that first pandemic spring to figure out how to move my courses to an online format. I bought a cheap plastic tablet and electronic stylus setup so that I could draw on a virtual whiteboard shared with my students over Zoom, but found the technology lacking, so I ended up messing around with various Apple Pencil–based applications until I found something that worked. I was also forced to finally master the Canvas course management software so that I could accept electronic assignment submissions. In isolation, these new tasks were not overwhelming in scale, but they arrived unexpectedly and accompanied by a sense of urgency. Many other knowledge workers had a similar experience. The pandemic didn't drown them in new work, but it did seem to suddenly inflate the quantity of overhead tax they were paying.

The shift to remote work also made collaboration somewhat less efficient, increasing the time required to satisfy the demands of this new overhead tax. If we're working in the same building, and I have a question for you about a project, I can wait until I see your office door is open and then swing by for an impromptu five-minute chat. If I'm working from home, by contrast, we might instead set up a Zoom meeting, which due to the format of most digital calendars will likely require that we set aside at least thirty minutes. "When we work remotely, this kind of ad-hoc coordination becomes harder to organize," I wrote in a 2020 article about the costs of remote work, "and decisions start to drag."

These increases in both the quantity and cost of overhead tax were modest. (I had to learn new technology for my college courses, but I didn't, for example, need to create whole new courses from scratch.) And yet these modest increases were enough to push many, like Jonathan Frostick, past the overhead tax tipping point, spiraling them into the all-consuming quantities of logistical overload that defined the worst moments of the Zoom Apocalypse. This observation is important not just for what it tells us about our work during the pandemic, but also for what it tells us about our work *right before* these disruptions arrived. When the shift toward remote work began in the spring of 2020, many knowledge workers had already pushed their workload right up to the threshold of the overhead tax tipping point, the maximum possible amount of administrative overhead that still allowed them to more or less keep up. All that was required to destabilize their professional lives was a final unexpected push. As the pandemic disruptions subsided and we escaped the Zoom Apocalypse, many seemed to have drifted right back to this same perilous edge, just barely able to get enough things done and fearing that they're one extra demand or emergency away from once again losing control.

It doesn't require an operations expert to conclude that this game of chicken with the overhead tax tipping point is a crazy way to arrange our professional lives. To make this more concrete, let's consider some simple numbers. Imagine that you produce reports that your company sells. Further, imagine it takes seven hours of core effort to complete a single report, and each report that you've committed to write generates one hour per day of overhead tax (emails, meetings, occupied mental space, and so on) until it's completed.* In this thought experiment, if you commit to just one report at a time, giving it your full mental attention until it's done before you agree to start working on another, you'll complete reports at the rate of one per day (assuming you work eight hours per day). If, on the other hand, you agree to take on four different reports simultaneously, the combined overhead tax of maintaining all four on your task list will eat up half your day in logistical wrangling, effectively doubling the time required to complete a single report. In this example, doing fewer things ends up producing more results.

The advantage of doing fewer things, however, is about more than just increasing the raw number of hours dedicated to useful activity; the *quality* of these hours also increases. When you approach a project without the hurried need to tend many barely contained

---

* A key property of overhead tax is that it tends to expand to fill as much time as it's provided. So long as a project is something that you've committed to, and it's not yet complete, it will tend to generate a continual tax in the form of check-in meetings, impromptu email conversations, and plain old mental space.

fires, you enjoy a more expansive sense of experimentation and possibility. Maybe you're able to identify a clever new business strategy, devise an elegant algorithm, or come up with a bold advertising campaign that would have eluded you in a more fragmented state of attention. There are boring physiological and neurological explanations for this effect involving the mind-constricting impacts of cortisol when your schedule becomes unrealistically full, or the time required to excite rich semantic connections among your brain's neurons. But we don't need science to convince us of something that we've all experienced directly: our brains work better when we're not rushing.

We've now refuted a common confusion about the first principle of slow productivity: it's easy to mistake "do fewer things" as a request to "accomplish fewer things." But this understanding gets things exactly backward. Whether your task list is overflowing or sparse, you're still working more or less the same number of hours each week. The size of your list affects only how usefully these hours produce results. It's here that we find the primary argument for why doing fewer things is as important for modern knowledge workers as it was for Jane Austen. It's not just because overload is exhausting and unsustainable and a miserable way to exist—though it certainly is—but because doing fewer things makes us better at our jobs; not only psychologically, but also economically and creatively. Focusing intensely on a small number of tasks, waiting to finish each before bringing on something new, is objectively a much better way to use our brains to produce valuable output.

But are such sparser workloads even possible anymore? So much of knowledge work culture seems built around juggling more and more work, with more and more "efficiency," that the idea of doing fewer things, even if logical in the abstract, seems an impossible goal to pursue in practice. Before we begin exploring specific strategies for implementing this principle, in other words, we must first convince ourselves that it's an approach that the modern workplace will even allow.

After first encountering the story of Jonathan Frostick and the broader Zoom Apocalypse trend he encapsulated, I found myself distracted by the central mystery of these events: How is it that so many knowledge workers end up with workloads calibrated to the exact edge of the overhead tax tipping point? One could imagine an alternative scenario in which most workers are far from that edge, easily able to absorb unexpected new commitments, or conversely, a scenario where workers constantly spiral past the tipping point in Frostick-style burnout. But this is not what we see. Most workers who are fortunate enough to exert some control over their efforts—such as knowledge workers, small-business entrepreneurs, or freelancers—tend to avoid taking on so much work that they crash and burn, but also tend to avoid working a reasonable amount. They exist at that point of maximum sustainable overhead tax that seems to represent the worst of all configurations, as it maintains the pain of having too much to do, but keeps this pain just manageable enough to avoid reform.

Much of the existing discussion I encountered about these issues adopted ideas from a traditional conflict theory framework that claims we are pushed toward overwork because an exploitative entity, such as a manager or business owner, is trying to extract as much value as possible from our labor. These frameworks, however, originally developed in the context of strictly controlled industrial manufacturing, and later expanded to include the hourly wage service sector, apply uneasily at best to the semiautonomy and ambiguity of knowledge work. If you toil at a computer screen for a living, tasks are not necessarily directly assigned to you by a stopwatch-wielding manager looking to hit a production target at all costs but are instead thrown in your direction more haphazardly, from all directions—colleagues, the HR department, clients. Furthermore, as we just established, the dynamics of cognitive labor are different from those of physical labor. In a factory, pushing employees to work longer shifts might be directly more profitable. In knowledge work, by contrast, pushing employees into larger workloads can decrease both the quantity and quality of what they produce. If our workloads were entirely determined by all-powerful managers looking to maximize profits, we might expect, as paradoxical as this sounds at first, to have *less* on our plates.

It is the acceptance of this fundamentally uncontrolled nature of knowledge work that provides a solution to our mystery: self-regulation. How do knowledge workers decide when to say no to the constant bombardment of incoming requests? In the modern office context, they tend to rely on stress as a default heuristic for moderation. If you turn down a Zoom meeting invitation, there's a social-capital cost, as you're causing some mild harm to a colleague and potentially signaling yourself to be uncooperative or a loafer. But, if you feel sufficiently stressed about your workload, this cost might become acceptable: you feel confident that you're close to becoming unsustainably busy, and this provides psychological cover to skip the Zoom. You need to feel sufficient personal distress to justify the distress saying no might generate in the other party.

The problem with deploying this stress heuristic, of course, is that you don't start turning away incoming tasks until you find yourself already creeping up to the edge of unsustainable workloads. It ensures that you'll remain permanently in this exhausting liminal space that immediately precedes the overhead tax tipping point. This is why so many knowledge workers feel vaguely overloaded all the time, and why we were so vulnerable to collapsing into full burnout when pushed by unexpected disruptions: the informal manner in which we manage our workloads ensures we always have dangerously too much to do.

This insight is good news for our quest to implement the first principle of slow productivity. If the source of our overwork is to some degree a side effect of the idiosyncratic manner in which we manage our obligations, then we can have hope that better options are possible. Indeed, in my reader survey conducted for this book, I came across numerous examples of knowledge workers in standard busy knowledge-work jobs who discovered not only that it's possible to do fewer things in their professional lives, but that in doing so, as predicted, they ended up both happier and better at their jobs.

A coach named Laura, for example, reported that she simplified her practice by reducing her offerings down to a few key services. "Since figuring this out," she told me, "my brain is calmer, the quality of my interactions is stronger, and my work quality is higher." As a result of this higher-quality work, she now makes the same amount of money working fewer hours. Ironically, as Laura admits, the original goal in doing less work was to find more balance with other parts of her life. The fact that she ended up making just as much money was a happy surprise.

A law professor named Jason told me a similar story about a beneficial decision to "narrow his focus." A year previously, he paused his "usual frenetic pace" of journal article writing to focus deeply on a single, important case in which he was retained as an expert witness. "The focus and attention I have given to my reports, and the preparation required to withstand hostile depositions and cross-examination, has helped me produce the best work of my career thus far," he said. "I have done some preliminary academic presentations on it, and I have never received such an engaged and impressed response to my work." Jason's career, in other words, is leaping forward due to his decision to hold back on growing his task list.

A teacher named Aurelia, fed up with the overload that's endemic in K–12 education, quietly adopted a clear rule: "I no longer do work that is not compensated and clearly expected as part of my job." Nothing bad ended up happening as a result of this new line in the sand. It turns out that a lot of the "nonsense" that was eating up her time wasn't really so urgent after all. An anonymous senior consultant told me about how his career turned around when his company put in place a policy that gave its consultants allotments of nonbillable hours that they could use for whatever they wanted. "This has been life changing," he explained. "I was able to learn and branch out into new areas . . . it reengaged me in the field . . . it has reminded me why I enjoy all this in the first place." A civil engineer manager named Nick walked away from an exhausting sixty-hour-a-week job for a thirty-hour-a-week role with much more clearly defined expectations, allowing him to maintain a more manageable workload. "I find that I'm able to produce nearly as much as before only working fifty percent of the hours because my focus is narrower," he explained with evident surprise.

We've established that overload is not fundamental to knowledge work. It's instead largely a side effect of the crude ways in which we self-manage our work volume. We further established that toiling at maximum capacity greatly reduces the rate at which we accomplish useful things, as it chokes our schedule in administrative kudzu and splinters our attention into fragments too small to support original thinking. What was true for Jane Austen in the eighteenth century is true for those who stare at computer screens in the twenty-first: doing fewer things is the key to producing good work.

This recognition, however, is not enough on its own to support the transformation of your professional life. The knowledge sector remains defined by the demands of pseudo-productivity. To the unenlightened, your commitment to do less might be received as laziness or diminished work ethic. A more careful and tactical approach is needed to successfully shift toward a Chawton cottage–style freedom in a working world buried in meeting invites and electronic messages. It's to these more concrete ideas that we now turn our attention.

Proposition: Limit the Big

In seeking inspiration for how to implement the first principle of slow productivity—to do fewer things—it makes sense to start with a famous example of professional simplification: mathematician Andrew Wiles's pursuit of Fermat's last theorem, a deceptively simple number theory problem first identified in the seventeenth century by the French polymath Pierre de Fermat that had resisted solutions for centuries.* As detailed in science writer Simon Singh's impressively researched book, *Fermat's Enigma*, the story of this theorem's eventual solution begins in dramatic fashion. The scene opens on a library in the 1960s. A ten-year-old Andrew Wiles comes across a book that introduces him to the theorem. He's entranced. "Here was a problem that I, a ten-year-old, could understand," he told Singh. "And I knew from that moment that I would never let it go. I had to solve it."

Jump forward to 1986. Wiles is now a mathematics professor at Princeton University, where he has distinguished himself as one of the stronger number theorists of his generation, having made an early breakthrough on the arithmetic of elliptic curves. It's here the

---

* For those who are interested, here is one of several equivalent statements of Fermat's last theorem: for every value of n greater than two, there are no three whole numbers a, b, and c that satisfy the following equation: $a^n + b^n = c^n$.

narrative receives a jolt of deus ex machina. Wiles learns that a fellow number theorist named Ken Ribet had established a surprising link between Fermat's puzzle and an obscure, highly technical claim known as the Taniyama-Shimura conjecture: solving this conjecture, Ribet demonstrated, would prove that Fermat's last theorem was also true.

Wiles is floored. The Taniyama-Shimura conjecture, as it turns out, draws heavily on elliptic curve theory. Wiles, who at the age of ten had declared he would one day solve Fermat's last theorem, had all of a sudden just become one of the most qualified people in the world to do so. "I was electrified. I knew that moment that the course of my life was changing," he said. "It meant that my childhood dream was now a respectable thing to work on. I just knew that I could never let that go."

What makes Andrew Wiles relevant to slow productivity is how he reacts to this fateful decision to focus all of his energy on this singular pursuit. As Singh summarizes, the young mathematician immediately began reducing his commitments:

> Wiles abandoned any work that was not directly relevant to proving Fermat's Last Theorem and stopped attending the never-ending round of conferences and colloquia. Because he still had responsibilities in the Princeton mathematics department, Wiles continued to attend seminars, lecture to undergraduates, and give tutorials. Whenever possible he would avoid the distractions of being a faculty member by working at home, where he could retreat into his attic study.

There remained, of course, the issue of publishing. A Princeton professor would be expected to produce papers. To avoid unwanted attention, Wiles devised what Singh labels "a cunning ploy." Throughout most of the early 1980s, Wiles had been working in the background on a "major piece" of research on elliptic curve theory that he had been preparing to publish in one large, head-turning manuscript. He now changed course. To buy time to work on Fermat's theorem, he decided to instead break up this nearly complete work into smaller pieces, publishing one short paper every six months or so. "This apparent productivity would convince his colleagues that he was still continuing with his usual research," explains Singh.

Wiles began serious work on Fermat's last theorem in 1986. For five years, he toiled in secret, often in his attic office, systematically avoiding larger projects and obligations. Starting in the early 1990s, as he got closer to a solution, he began to once again attend some elliptic curve conferences to refresh his mathematical toolbox with new techniques. He then landed a position as a visiting research professor at Oxford, which simplified his efforts to focus. (These appointments, by design, have few obligations beyond thinking deeply on hard problems.) Finally, in 1993, eight years after he began his quest, Wiles presented his completed proof of the Taniyama-Shimura conjecture in a series of lectures at the Isaac Newton Institute at Cambridge. For his final lecture, members of the media, tipped off by conference attendees about what was coming, filled the back of the room. When he got to the end of his proof, Wiles quipped, "I think I'll stop here." Then the camera flashes began.

Assuming you're not a tenured mathematics professor, the specific actions Andrew Wiles took to simplify his workload are likely not that relevant. What is useful for our discussion, however, is the general approach he deployed. To prepare himself to focus on a single large and meaningful project, Wiles limited large pursuits and commitments that would compete for his time. Crucially, he was systematic in this reduction. He didn't resolve, in some generic fashion, to try to take on less; he instead put in place specific rules (e.g., no conferences), habits (e.g., work from home as much as possible), and even ploys (e.g., trickling out his already completed research)—all directed toward minimizing the number of big items tugging at his attention.

This first proposition suggests that you follow Andrew Wiles's example and implement a systematic plan for limiting significant commitments in your own professional life. There are many ways to pursue this goal. In the strategies that follow, I'll outline a specific approach that I've found to be particularly useful: applying limits at different scales of work at the same time, from your overarching missions, to your ongoing projects, to your daily goals.

Intentional limits set concurrently at all three of these scales are more likely to succeed than focusing on just one scale in isolation. If you have multiple major professional missions, for example, you'll struggle to limit the pool of ongoing projects they generate. Similarly, if you have too many ongoing projects, you'll struggle to prevent your daily schedule from becoming overstuffed. What follows, then, are three limit strategies, one for each of these three scales.

LIMIT MISSIONS

The term *mission* can sound grandiose. For our purposes, we'll demote it to a more pragmatic definition: any ongoing goal or service that directs your professional life. Andrew Wiles had a mission to solve Fermat's last theorem. Winning grants, effectively managing HR requests, producing new creative briefs, and crafting elegant computer programs are all missions as well. They're what ultimately decide where you aim your attention in your job. It's easy to let your collection of missions expand, as the embrace of a big new goal can be exciting in the moment. But missions, once adopted, demand effort. If your professional life is top heavy, you'll unavoidably face an onerous workload. Any attempt to succeed with our first principle of slow productivity, therefore, must begin with the reduction of your main objectives.

It's hard to specify the optimal number of missions, but generally, less is better than more. There's a romance to focusing on a single pursuit, but this level of simplicity is typically accessible only to the most purely creative fields—Hemingway at Key West, banging out his morning pages on his Corona typewriter. Two or three missions are more tractable and still quite minimalist. When I graduated from college, for example, with a major in computer science and a book deal with Random House, I decided to keep my work intensely focused on just these two missions: academic research and writing. This lasted until I was hired as an assistant professor, at which point I had to add a third mission dedicated to servicing the necessary nonresearch aspects of academic life, including class preparation and student supervision. Three missions still feel compatible with slow productivity, especially if I'm careful to control it (see the next proposition for more on that), but, if I'm honest, I'm nostalgic for the simplicity of two, and salivate over the idea of one.

Moving in the other direction, it's hard to maintain five or more missions without the feeling you're drowning in unavoidable work. This might sound like a lot of objectives to take on, but it's easier than you might imagine to allow your commitment count to grow over time. My friend Jenny Blake, for example, writes in her 2022 book, *Free Time*, about how her small consulting and training business kept expanding until, one day, exhausted by the demands of work, she looked up and realized she was supporting more than ten different sources of income, which she described as "legacies from years of experimenting." No amount of clever time management or streamlining tactics can keep the work required to maintain ten missions tractable.

After Blake began fantasizing about "winning the lottery or burning it all down," she realized she had to simplify if she had any hope of achieving a sustainable and meaningful professional life. She slashed her income streams and reduced her staff to only three part-time employees. She now works, on average, twenty hours a week and takes off two full months each year for vacation. It's likely, of course, that Blake would be making more money if she hustled to support more missions. When you're enjoying twenty-hour workweeks, however, it's hard to care too much about such possibilities.

LIMIT PROJECTS

Missions require that you initiate "projects," which is my term for any work-related initiative that cannot be completed in a single session. Some projects you complete once and then are done, such as updating the sales copy on a product website. Other projects are ongoing, meaning they unfold without any clear stopping point, such as answering support queries from clients. Projects create many of the concrete tasks that take up your time during the day. It follows that limiting them is critical to limiting your overall work volume.

A crude approach to accomplishing this goal is to adopt the persona of someone who is eccentric and unresponsive, eventually driving your colleagues to redirect their requests and assignments elsewhere. In my book *Deep Work*, I pointed toward the Nobel Prize–winning theoretical physicist Richard Feynman as a canonical example of this approach. In *Deep Work*, I highlighted the following excerpt from a 1981 interview Feynman, then a professor at Caltech, gave to the BBC show *Horizon*:

> To do real good physics work, you do need absolute solid lengths of time . . . it needs a lot of concentration . . . if you have a job administrating anything, you don't have the time. So I have invented another myth for myself: that I'm irresponsible. I'm actively irresponsible. I tell everybody I don't do anything.

Even for someone as devotedly eccentric as Feynman, however, maintaining this veneer of antisociality is demanding. I neglected to mention in *Deep Work*, for example, that a half decade after his *Horizon* interview, Feynman's protective shield of irresponsibility was pierced when his former student, William Graham, then the acting director of NASA, called Feynman and persuaded him to join the presidential commission on the space shuttle *Challenger* disaster. Feynman ultimately helped identify the cause of the *Challenger* explosion: the shuttle's rubber O-ring seals lost their elasticity when cooled below a certain temperature. Feynman's famous demonstration of this problem during the commission's televised hearings, in which he plunged an O-ring into a glass of ice water, became iconic, and attracted the aging physicist a new round of late-in-life celebrity.

For all the success of his participation in this commission, however, it's undeniable that it represents a failure of Feynman's best-laid plans to avoid extraneous projects in his professional life. "Irresponsibility requires eternal vigilance," Feynman told the *Los Angeles Times* in a 1986 profile. "And I failed! I wasn't careful enough when this presidential commission thing came up. I flunked my own principle." A plan to simply become too unpleasant to be bothered, it seems, isn't sustainable. There are only so many times you can offer an unqualified no without either losing your job or being sidelined as an unreliable curmudgeon.

This leaves us with a more nuanced option for limiting projects: appeal to the hard but unimpeachable reality of your actual available time. If someone asks you to do something, and you appeal to some vague sense of busyness to get out of it, you're unlikely to consistently succeed. "We're all busy," they might reply, "but I really need you to do this for me." If you instead have a reputation as someone who is careful about managing their time and can quantify your busyness more concretely, you have a better chance of avoiding the new work. When you say, "I don't see any really significant swaths of open time to work on something like this for at least three weeks, and in the meantime, I have five other projects competing for my schedule," it's hard for someone to rebut you, unless they're willing to challenge your calculations, or demand that you expand your working hours to accommodate their specific request.

To gain this credibility, I recommend, at first, when considering a new project, you estimate how much time it will require and then *go find that time and schedule it on your calendar*. Block off the hours as you would for a meeting. If you're unable to find enough blank spaces in your schedule in the near future to easily fit the work, then you don't have enough time for it. Either decline the project, or cancel something else to make room. The power of this approach is that you're dealing with the reality of your time, not a gut feeling about how busy you are at the moment.

You don't have to continue pre-scheduling your projects in this manner indefinitely. After you've executed this strategy for a while, you'll develop an instinct for roughly how many commitments you can maintain at any point without overtaxing your time. Going forward, it becomes sufficient to just track your current project tally, and reject new work once you pass your limit—making adjustments as needed, of course, for unusually busy periods.

Although this approach is designed to prevent you from accepting more work than you have time to handle, filling every available minute of your workday with projects can still lead to a level of busyness that's incompatible with slow productivity, even if it is feasible to execute. This can be solved by limiting the time you make available for project work (remember Jenny Blake's twenty-hour workweeks) as well as by padding your estimates to make sure you have more than enough time to complete, without frenzy or rush, whatever work you do accept. We'll elaborate on these types of ideas in the next chapter, which focuses on the principle of working at a natural pace. For now, what's important with this strategy is that you maintain clarity and control over your schedule, and deploy it to keep your workload reasonable, regardless of how you define this condition. There exists a myth that it's hard to say no, whether to someone else or to your own ambition. The reality is that saying no isn't so bad if you have hard evidence that it's the only reasonable answer.

LIMIT DAILY GOALS

We've arrived at the smallest scale of work that we'll consider for our limiting strategies: the projects you decide to make progress on during the current day. My recommendation here is simple: work on at most one project per day. To clarify, I don't intend for this single daily project to be your *only* work for the day. You'll likely also have meetings to attend, emails to answer, and administrative nonsense to subdue (we'll talk more about these smaller tasks in the upcoming proposition about containing the small). But when it comes to expending efforts on important, bigger initiatives, stay focused on just one target per day.

I learned this principle of daily project limits from my doctoral adviser at MIT, one of the founders of the study of distributed algorithm theory, and a massively productive scholar. She was often incredulous at my attempts to switch back and forth between multiple academic papers, or to combine book writing with computer science thinking in the same day. She preferred to get lost in a single project at a time, obsessing over it until she could release it fully to move on to what came next. I was convinced that the *slowness* of working on just one important thing per day would hold me back. Fueled by the impatient ambition of youth, I wanted to make progress on as many things as possible at the same time.

I was, of course, wrong and she was right. There's a calibrated steadiness to working on just one major initiative a day. Real progress accrues, while anxiety is subdued. This pace might seem slow in the moment, but zooming out to consider the results that eventually accrue over many months reveals the narrowness of this concern. I was too young to appreciate this reality as a graduate student in my twenties, but I for sure recognize its wisdom today.

Proposition: Contain the Small

Benjamin Franklin might seem an unusual choice to feature in a book about slow productivity, as his work ethic was famously grinding. In his autobiography, for example, Franklin talked about gaining notice for his fledgling Philadelphia print shop by making a show of working longer hours than his competitors, often plying his presses until midnight or beyond. "This industry, visible to our neighbors, began to give us character and credit," he wrote. After establishing his core printing business, Franklin expanded his commercial activity by publishing a newspaper, *The Pennsylvania Gazette*, which he helped grow, in part, by taking on a thankless and demanding position as the postmaster of Philadelphia, which gave him early access to news items.

Three years after introducing the *Gazette*, Franklin then moved into books and began publishing his *Poor Richard's Almanack*, which also quickly became popular. In search of even more revenue, Franklin set up a pair of franchise versions of his print shop in other locations: the first in South Carolina, and the second in New York City. These complicated arrangements required Franklin to install a printer to run each operation locally, while he provided capital and expertise in exchange for splitting the profits. During this period, Franklin began to keep a daily checklist of cardinal virtues he desired to observe. Not surprisingly, one of these virtues was "industry," which Franklin defined in his autobiography by the resolutions to "lose no time" and to "be always employed in something useful." One can assume that this particular row on his list consistently received his check marks.

This view of Franklin as the patron saint of busyness, however, misses a more nuanced story. While it's true that his professional career began in a state of overload, it didn't stay that way. Biographer H. W. Brands points out that as Franklin ground his way through his thirties, he began to burn out. "Part of Franklin's problem," writes Brands, "was that he was starting to stretch himself thin." It's here that Franklin made an unexpected and underreported swing toward slow productivity.

At the core of Franklin's discovery of slowness is a touch of serendipity. It began when Franklin decided to open a third printing franchise, this one to be located in the West Indies, and run by a British printer's assistant named David Hall. Arriving in Philadelphia in 1744, Hall disrupted these plans when he fell sick with jaundice, likely caused by a case of hepatitis caught on his long trip across the Atlantic from London. Franklin made the fateful decision to employ David Hall in his own Philadelphia shop while waiting for him to recover. Franklin was so impressed with Hall's skill, however, that he ended up scrapping the West Indies plan, deciding instead to keep his new employee permanently local. As Brands writes:

> Hall became Franklin's foreman, handling the affairs of the shop with a skill and efficiency that not even the fastidious Franklin could fault. The printing business grew more profitable to its owner, yet he had to devote less time to it than ever.

No longer weighed down by all the administrative minutiae required to run a complicated business, Franklin increasingly turned his attention toward loftier and more engaging projects. In the first four years after Hall's arrival, Franklin popularized his highly efficient woodburning stove, organized a citizen militia in Philadelphia, and started the American Philosophical Society.

Then, in 1748, Franklin made a major move to cement this

newly uncovered free time, when he promoted David Hall from foreman to full partner. Franklin passed off all the details of running his business interests to Hall, with whom he would split the profits. As Brands points out, this move significantly reduced Franklin's potential wealth. He gave up not only half his annual profits, but also the further growth of his business that would have resulted if Franklin, a talented businessman, had remain engaged with its operation, coming up with new schemes and pushing for new markets.

But Franklin was happy with this trade of money for time to pursue more meaningful projects. Indeed, a certain joy in this newfound freedom infuses Franklin's correspondence from this period. "I am settling my old accounts and hope soon to be quite a master of my own time," he wrote to a friend in London in 1748, before elaborating:

> I am in a fair way of having no other *tasks* than such as I shall like to give my self, and of enjoying what I look upon as a great happiness, leisure to read, study, make experiments, and converse at large . . . on such points as may produce something for the common benefit of mankind, uninterrupted by the little cares and fatigues of business.

Franklin's optimistic predictions for the potential of life without "tasks" and the "little cares and fatigues of business" proved accurate. In 1748, he began an obsessive focus on the theory behind electricity, a little-understood phenomenon that Franklin had first encountered a year earlier during a demonstration in Boston.

Freed from his normal administrative load, Franklin made immediate progress in the field. In a remarkably short span of just a few years, Franklin introduced a theory of positive and negative flow, invented the battery, and built a rudimentary electric motor.

Most consequential, however, was his theory of lightning as an electrical phenomenon, which not only offered a clear naturalistic explanation for these bolts from the heavens, but also identified a simple solution to the damage they so frequently caused: the lightning rod. When Franklin's theory was validated in a concurrent set of experiments—one conducted by a set of French researchers mounting a rod to a tower during a storm, and the other, Franklin's famous flying of a kite—he was catapulted to worldwide fame. Soon after, in part owing to his sudden celebrity, Franklin was elected to the Pennsylvania Assembly, thrusting him, for the first time, into provincial politics in a serious way. We all know what happened next.

What makes Benjamin Franklin's colonial midlife crisis notable to a modern audience is his general belief that taming the impact of small details in your professional life opens up space to pursue bigger goals. Franklin may have been an early observer of this idea, but he was hardly the last. Here, for example, is the Scottish crime novelist Ian Rankin, describing the onslaught of the mundane that so often keeps him from his writing: "The phone rings, the doorbell sounds, there's shopping to be done or an urgent email demanding a reply." He refers to these distracted days as "wading through suet." Rankin's solution—his personal version of hiring

David Hall—is to retreat to an isolated house on the northeast coast of Scotland, in the town of Cromarty, on the Black Isle. As he elaborates:

> When I go up north, I write in a room at the top of the house. If it's cold, I'll light the wood-burner. When the sun's out, I often go for a walk and do my writing in the late afternoon or evening. When I hit a wall or a problem, a walk often brings sudden illumination.

Edith Wharton was also concerned about the intrusion of the small on her bigger pursuits. During the nine-year period when she lived at the Mount, her expansive estate in the Berkshires, Wharton insisted on a rigid routine to protect her writing from the distractions of her frequent visitors. From when she awoke until at least 11:00 a.m., she would sit up in her bed, working longhand on a writing board balanced on her knees. By some reports, she would drop finished pages to the ground to be later collected by a secretary to type up. Guests were taught to entertain themselves until lunchtime, as Wharton was not to be disturbed. "The slightest interruption in the household routine completely de-rails me," she wrote in a 1905 letter.

I enjoy collecting these stories of glamorous defenses against distraction. I find them aspirational, even if they remain, in their specifics, often laughably unobtainable. Hiring David Hall, retreating to a house on a remote Scottish isle, or leaving chores to a staff while you write in bed is not a suggestion that most of us can easily replicate.* The underlying motivation driving these stories, however, shouldn't be dismissed. Small tasks, in sufficient quantity, can act like productivity termites, destabilizing the whole foundation of what you're trying to build. It's worth going to great lengths to tame them.

With this goal in mind, in the pages that follow, I present a collection of more practical strategies designed to help you gain mastery over the small obligations in your professional life. This topic of taming tasks is one I've tackled before. In my book *Deep Work*, for example, I included a chapter titled "Drain the Shallows," which explored this theme. In it, I recommended better organizing your hours using time blocking—a strategy, as it turns out, that was originally pioneered by Franklin—so that tasks could be better separated from deeper efforts. I also suggested writing more structured emails to minimize unnecessary back-and-forth messaging, an objective I elaborate in much greater detail in a follow-up book I published a half decade later titled *A World Without Email*. Surrounding these books are numerous pages of articles and hours of podcast discussions where I've also tackled this topic in depth.

The strategies I've collected here represent a greatest hits of sorts, culled from my years of experience battling distracting task lists.

---

* For example, for a sobering critical take on the specific circumstances and privileges required to support Benjamin Franklin's rise, I recommend Jill Lepore's 2013 National Book Awards Finalist, *Book of Ages: The Life and Opinions of Jane Franklin*. Lepore details how Benjamin Franklin's sister Jane shared a similar intelligence and ambition to her famous brother but, due to the demands on women of that class in that time (Jane raised *twelve* children!), had no viable outlet for her talents.

This advice is unified by the notion of *containment*. Several of these ideas focus on containing the overhead tax of tasks you cannot avoid tackling. In many cases, it's not the actual execution of a small commitment that generates distraction, it's instead the cognitive effort required to remember it, to worry about it, and to eventually find time for it in your schedule. If you can minimize this preparatory effort, you can contain the impact of the task itself. Other ideas will focus on containing tasks by preventing them from arriving on your lists in the first place. In both cases, the goal is limiting damage.

Slow productivity requires that you free yourself from the constraints of the small so that you can invest more meaningfully in the big. This is a messy, detail-oriented conflict, largely fought on the battleground of old-fashioned productivity tactics and systems. But it's a battle that must be fought if you hope to, as Benjamin Franklin lauded, become the master of your own time. So, let's get into it . . .

PUT TASKS ON AUTOPILOT

In my twenties, when my writing focused on student advice, I used to frequently recommend an organizational strategy called an *autopilot schedule*. The idea was to assign regularly occurring classwork to specific times on specific days, and sometimes even specific locations, each week. Maybe you always do your English lit reading after your 10:00 a.m. class on Tuesdays and Thursdays, using the same table, on the same floor of the same nearby library. This strategy worked because it countered many students' default tendency to work only on what was urgently due. It's rare the undergraduate, for example, who spontaneously thinks, "Maybe I should get started working on that problem set three days in advance." But if this task is on his autopilot schedule for the current day, he will, without much consideration, simply work on it. "Once you get to the point where your regular work is getting done with minimum of thinking," I wrote in one of my early articles on this topic, "you've hit that low-stress sweet spot where you can start turning your attention to the bigger things."

As I later pivoted my writing away from student issues, the autopilot schedule faded into the background as I focused on more office-specific tools, like time blocking and email protocols. Recently, however, as the administrative demands of my own job continue to expand, I've begun once again to experiment with this strategy. In the context of knowledge work, it turns out, autopilot schedules provide an effective means to contain tasks. Instead of setting regular times each week for completing school assignments, you can set times for accomplishing specific categories of regularly occurring tasks. A freelancer, for example, might schedule sending invoices for Monday morning, while a professor might schedule reviewing grant reports for Fridays, right after lunch. Once you get used to accomplishing a specific type of task at the same times on the same days, the overhead required for their execution plummets.

A key refinement to support this task-centric version of autopilot scheduling is to leverage rituals and locations. If you can connect a regularly recurring task block to a specific location, perhaps paired with a little ritual that helps initiate your efforts, you're more likely to fall into a regular rhythm of accomplishing this work. Returning to our professor example, perhaps on Fridays she plans to always eat lunch at the same dining hall in the student center, and then once done, walk across the nearby campus green (a ritual) to the same carrel in the same small library (location), where she sits down and works through her grant reports. Maybe after she's done, she returns to the student center to grab a coffee to bring back to her office (another ritual). This combination of ritual and location makes it more likely that our hypothetical professor will actually review those reports, week after week, without actual thinking much about it.

I recommend capturing as many categories of regular tasks as possible into an increasingly elaborate autopilot schedule: when you review client request; when you check in on the contractors updating your website; when you prep for meetings; when you read emails or update project management websites. Containing tasks is not about escaping the small. It's instead about making these efforts as painless as possible. Seeking, as I once put it, that "low-stress sweet spot."

SYNCHRONIZE

In the fall of 2020, I published a long piece for *The New Yorker* titled "The Rise and Fall of Getting Things Done." It opened on the story of Merlin Mann, a web designer and freelance project manager who found himself in the early 2000s increasingly overwhelmed by his work. It was at this point that he discovered David Allen's Getting Things Done (GTD) methodology. Allen's systematic approach to organizing lengthy task lists was exactly what

Mann felt he needed. He started a blog called *43 Folders*—a reference to the "tickler file" technique described by Allen—to catalog his growing enthusiasm for the system.* "Believe me, if you keep finding that the water of your life has somehow run onto the floor," Mann wrote in an early post, "GTD may be just the drinking glass you need to get things back together."

43 Folders grew to become one of the internet's most popular productivity blogs, leading Mann to quit his job as a project manager to work on the site full time. What makes his story interesting, however, is not only his rise, but also his subsequent fall. Roughly three years after starting *43 Folders*, Mann grew disillusioned with the promises of systems like GTD to transform work. These styles of productivity hacks, he wrote, didn't end up making him feel "more competent, stable, and alive." He refocused *43 Folders* away from pure productivity and toward the woollier goal of producing better creative work. Then he stopped posting altogether.

There are many explanations for Mann's disillusionment with detailed task management systems like GTD. The one I want to highlight here is perhaps the most fundamental: they didn't work. To be fair, they weren't entirely ineffective. Moving obligations out of your mind and into trusted systems—the foundation of GTD—

---

* The tickler file was a popular analog organizational strategy that was popularized by David Allen, but not invented by him. The idea is to have one folder for every day of the current month as well as one folder for each of the remaining months. You can then file relevant papers on the day of the current month you need them, or if you don't need them until later, in the folder for the month when you will return to them. The system requires thirty-one *day* folders and twelve *month* folders, which sums to forty-three total folders.

will make you less anxious and more organized. When I interviewed Mann, for example, he told me he still relies on GTD-inspired ideas for managing household chores, emphasizing that he didn't want to waste even a moment of mental energy on trying to remember to clean out his cat's litter box.

But systems like GTD, though helpful, were not able to really solve the issues of anxious overload that began to afflict knowledge workers like Mann in recent decades. The mismatch can be found in GTD's focus on stand-alone tasks. In Allen's system, obligations are reduced to concrete "next actions," which are added to expansive lists, categorized into different work "contexts." The practitioner simply references the list corresponding to their current context and begins cranking through the enumerated actions, one after another.

Starting in the 1990s, however, a lot of the activity that began dominating the attention of knowledge workers like Mann wasn't the execution of discrete tasks, but instead interactions with others *about* these tasks. The introduction of personal computers, followed soon after by electronic communication tools like email, transformed office collaboration into an ongoing, haphazard bazaar of asynchronous, back-and-forth messaging—a colleague asks you to handle something, you reply to clarify what he means, you then write another colleague to gather the needed information, but based on her response, you realize you don't fully understand the task, so you send a new message to the original requester, and so on. Multiply these drawn-out interactions by dozens of concurrent open loops, and soon you're spending most of your time managing conversations, not executing individual tasks. David Allen's carefully organized lists don't help the project manager who must reply to dozens of emails an hour.

From a slow productivity perspective, however, there's good news embedded in this otherwise discouraging account. If much of your perceived busyness comes from talking *about* tasks instead of actually executing them, you might be less overloaded than you realize. In other words, if you can reduce the footprint of these conversations, the pile of actual, concrete obligations that remains might not be so forbidding.

A direct strategy for reducing collaboration overhead is to replace asynchronous communication with real-time conversations. Consider my earlier example in which an ambiguous request from a colleague led to a long thread of back-and-forth messaging involving three different parties. If all three people were instead in the same room or video call at the same time, the task could have been perfectly clarified in just a few minutes of discussion. Arranging these conversations, however, is tricky. There's a reason why the saying *this meeting could have been an email* has entrenched itself as a workplace meme in recent years. If every task generates its own meeting, you'll end up trading a crowded inbox for a calendar crowded with meetings—a fate that is arguably just as dire.

The right balance can be found in using office hours: regularly scheduled sessions for quick discussion that can be used to resolve many different issues. Set aside the same thirty to sixty minutes every afternoon, and advertise this time to your colleagues and clients. Make it clear that you're always available during this period—your door is open, Zoom activated, Slack channels monitored, phone on—to chat about any and all relevant questions or requests. If someone sends you an ambiguous message, instead of letting it instigate yet another stretched-out volley of back-and-forth missives, reply, "Happy to help! Grab me during one of my upcoming office hours and we'll figure out the details."

This approach can also be adapted for teams in the form of a related strategy that I call docket-clearing meetings. Like office hours, these meetings happen at the same times on the same days, each week. Unlike office hours, they're attended by your entire team. During these sessions, your team churns through any pending tasks that require collaboration or clarification. The group moves through the tasks one at a time, figuring out for each what exactly needs to be done, who is working on it, and what information they need from others. An easy way to organize these sessions is to maintain a shared document of tasks to discuss. Team members can add items to the list as they come up in between meetings. One thirty-minute docket-clearing session can save a team from hours of highly distracting inbox checking and back-and-forth emailing.

It's hard to overemphasize the sense of relief granted by these two simple synchronization methods. When you separate work from the ad hoc conversations that surround it, what you're left with might not be all that intimidating. Merlin Mann discovered that even highly technical task management systems couldn't banish the sense of overload increasingly afflicting twenty-first-century office workers. The cure isn't to be found in smarter task systems, but instead in a return to something simpler, and more human: regular conversation.

MAKE OTHER PEOPLE WORK MORE

In another productivity-themed *New Yorker* article, this one published in early 2022, I offered a critique of the lack of rules or systems surrounding how tasks are identified and assigned in most knowledge work settings. We just fire up our inboxes, send out meeting invites, and rock and roll: everyone flinging new requests and questions toward everyone else.

When I was writing this article, I worried that people were so used to this culture of ad hoc task assignment that it would be hard for them to accept the idea that alternatives were even possible, so I decided to slip into my piece a purposefully over-the-top suggestion. My goal was to raise the ire of the reader, to make them react dismissively—"that could never work"—but then, in the process of convincing themselves that my suggestion was preposterous, perhaps find themselves questioning the status quo.

Here's what I wrote:

> Imagine everyone on your team puts aside one hour a day for completing small tasks and answering quick questions. Further imagine that they each post a shared document containing a sign-up sheet for a day's block, including only a limited number of slots. If you want someone on your team to, say, give you his availability for an upcoming client visit, you must find a free slot in which to record this request. He'll then see it and give you an answer during that day's administrative block—freeing him from the burden of having to manage all of these obligations in a single, overwhelming pile of unstructured urgency.

Part of what makes this thought experiment satisfying is that it reduces the painful asymmetry inherent in task assignment. Instead of allowing colleagues to effortlessly lob requests in your direction like hand grenades, leaving you to clean up the mess generated by their productivity-shredding shrapnel, they must now do more work themselves before they can commandeer your attention.

In general, strategies that require people to do more work can prove effective for containing tasks. Consider, for example, a more palatable version of my *New Yorker* suggestion that I call the reverse task list. It works as follows: Create a public task list for each of the major categories of tasks you tackle in your job. You can use a shared document for this purpose. (If you're feeling more advanced, a shared Trello board is perhaps even better.) When someone asks you to take on some small obligation, direct them to add it themselves to the relevant shared task list; writing it, for example, into the shared doc, or creating a new card for it on the shared Trello board. Critically, make it clear that *all* of the information you'll need to complete the task should be included in their entry.

Reverse task lists require people to spend more time specifying exactly what they need from you, which simplifies the later execution of their requests. You can also use these public lists to keep people updated on the status of the tasks you're currently handling, saving them from having to bother you with "How's it going?" messages. Finally, these lists clearly communicate your current workload. If a colleague encounters an overstuffed reverse task list, they might think twice about giving you something new to do.

Another strategy along these lines is to introduce processes that require your colleagues or clients to do more of the work associated with a given task. Imagine that you're an office manager tasked with supporting a team at a consulting firm. A common chore you might face is approving your team members' travel reimbursement forms. The default approach for accomplishing this task might be to have them email you forms they need approved, leaving you to print, sign, scan, and then submit them to payroll for processing.

An alternative is to announce a custom-built process that requires your team to do (slightly) more of this work before involving you. For example, maybe you set up two mail sorters outside your office door: one for new forms and one for signed forms. A team member who needs a reimbursement request signed must print it and put it in the first sorter outside your office. On Thursday mornings, you go through the forms in the first sorter, sign them, and then move them to the second sorter. It's now the responsibility of the relevant individuals to come back to your office, collect their signed forms, scan them, and submit them, cc'ing you on the message so you have a record. From the perspective of those requesting the reimbursement, this process adds a small amount of extra work into their life, but not enough that they'll notice or really care—as each individual submits these requests only occasionally. If anything, they might appreciate that there's such a clear policy. You as the office manager, however, have significantly reduced the overhead required to process dozens of such incoming requests each month.

At first, these strategies for making the burden of task assignments more symmetric can feel self-indulgent. You might even worry that others will be offended by your brashness. In reality, however, if you're diplomatic in your phrasing, and deploy sufficient self-deprecation, you can introduce these systems without attracting too much ire. Indeed, your peers might end up appreciating the added structure, as it provides clarity about how or when their requested work will actually be accomplished.

In general, people are often too focused on their own problems to care about how you're solving your own. Remember that deliberately provocative suggestion from my *New Yorker* essay? The one designed to generate headshaking disbelief from my readers? Not a single person wrote me to say I was going too far. Perhaps it was less radical than I assumed.

AVOID TASK ENGINES

It's natural to focus on taming the pile of tasks you've already built up. Equally effective containment strategies, however, can be found upstream in your workflow, before obligations are generated in the first place. The following such strategy, for example, can be surprisingly effective in reducing your task burden: When selecting new projects, assess your options by the number of weekly requests, questions, or small chores you expect the project to generate. Prioritize options that minimize this number. Most people focus on the difficulty of a project, or the total amount of time it might require. But once you understand the havoc wreaked by an overstuffed to-do list, it makes sense that the task footprint of a project should be taken just as seriously.

To make this more concrete, imagine a sales director trying to decide between two projects: writing a detailed report on how a new technology will affect the market, or organizing a one-day client conference. At first glance, the conference seems like an appealing choice. For one thing, it has a definitive event date, after which it's done, whereas the report might require many weeks of work to complete. Organizing the conference is also simpler in the sense that it doesn't require hard thinking, while the report will require the mastery of complicated information and the development of confident predictions.

And yet, in this scenario, I would definitely choose the report option for a simple reason: it will generate many fewer tasks. To organize the conference will require endless coordination with different clients, as well as the need to arrange room rentals and expert speakers, not to mention the hassle of catering, answering logistical questions, and so on. There will be last-minute issues to resolve and countless back-and-forth exchanges—with each obligation demanding its own slice of your mental energy. The client conference, in other words, is a *task engine*—an efficient generator of numerous urgent small things to do.

The market report, on the other hand, represents a different type of energy investment. It will require regular long blocks of time in which you must gather data, process it, and reflect on what it all means. This will be mentally demanding and, at times, perhaps tedious. But it will generate very few urgent small tasks and therefore make few demands on your attention outside of the blocks of time you've already set aside to work on it. Writing the report might not be easy, but the decision to choose it over the task engine represented by the messy event organization project should be.

SPEND MONEY

In the last section, as part of our discussion about limiting major work commitments, I introduced my friend Jenny Blake, who slashed the income streams pursued by her company from more than ten to a handful. Another thing that caught my attention about Jenny was the pride she clearly took in her professional software subscriptions. As she writes in her book *Free Time*, one of the steps she took to reconfigure her business toward a slow productivity model was to spend more money on "going pro" with useful software services, instead of, as she put it, "squeezing everything I could out of their freemium editions."

Jenny sent me a spreadsheet of every software subscription she maintains for her business, including its monthly cost. She wasn't kidding about her commitment to going pro with these tools. The sheet includes over fifty paid services, from Calendly to DocuSign to the professional version of Zoom, adding up to roughly $2,400 a month in subscription fees. There's a good reason, however, for this expense: these professional software services eliminate or simplify administrative work. Jenny's investing serious money, in other words, to seriously reduce the size of her task list.

From the context of slow productivity, investments of this type make a lot of sense. The more you can tame the small commitments pulling at your attention, the more sustainably and effectively you can work on things that matter. There are, of course, many options beyond software services for trading your money for reduced task lists. I know many entrepreneurs who reclaim a substantial amount of time by hiring and training "operations managers" to take on more of their daily details of running their businesses. I wouldn't be able to reasonably fit my podcast into my schedule, for example, if not for the producer I hired to come to my studio on recording days and take care of all the details surrounding the release of each week's episode. I could do all of this work on my own. Indeed, I used to when the show was new. But I learned from experience that the number of annoying details this generates is sufficiently high that if I had to keep handling it myself, I'd probably have given up on the show altogether.

Hiring professional service providers is another effective investment for keeping your task lists contained. Returning to my own example, I pay an accountant to manage my books, a professional agency to handle everything related to my podcast advertising, a web consultant to keep all of my online properties humming, and a lawyer to answer the many small questions that pop up in the normal course of running my writing-related business. Every effective entrepreneur I know shares a similar commitment to paying people who know what they're doing so they don't have to do the work, at a lower level of quality, all by themselves.

In the short term, all of this costs money. If your company is new, or your income still modest, it can be unnerving to see a nontrivial percent of these earnings go right back out the door. But in the long term, this off-loading of the small can provide the mental space needed to make the types of large breakthroughs, and produce the type of value, that will make these monthly expenses suddenly seem trivial in scope. Don't spend more than you can afford. But recognize that a practitioner of slow productivity cannot afford to spend nothing.

Interlude: What about Overwhelmed Parents?

Early in her 2014 book, *Overwhelmed: How to Work, Love, and Play When No One Has the Time*, Brigid Schulte, a journalist and mother of two, summarizes her experience as a working parent:

> I have baked Valentine's cupcakes until 2 a.m. and finished writing stories at 4 a.m. when all was quiet and I finally had unbroken time to concentrate. I have held what I hope were professional-sounding interviews sitting on the floor in the hall outside my kids' dentist's office. . . . Some appliance is always broken. My to-do list never ends. I have yet to do a family budget after meaning to for nearly twenty years. The laundry lies in such a huge, perpetually unfolded mound that my daughter has taken a dive in it and gone for a swim.

The first principle of slow productivity provides what is ostensibly professional advice. Working on fewer things can paradoxically produce *more* value in the long term: overload generates an untenable quantity of nonproductive overhead. But for working parents like Brigid Schulte, the call to do fewer things also resonates on a more personal level. One of the more insidious side effects of pseudo-productivity in the knowledge sector is the manner in which it forces individuals to manage tensions between work and life all on their own. If you toil in a factory, and your employer wants you to put in twelve-hour days, this demand will be clearly specified in a labor contract, in black and white, in a form that can be pointed to and argued about. Your union can fight back. Concrete counterproposals can be made. If needed, perhaps legislation can be passed, such as the 1938 Fair Labor Standards Act, which required extra pay for work beyond forty hours a week.

Under a pseudo-productivity regime, by contrast, such demands are more implicit and self-reinforced. You're judged on how much total work you visibly tackle from a never-ending supply of available tasks, but no one is going to tell you specifically how much is enough—that's up to you. *Good luck!* This reality requires parents—and more specifically moms, who often shoulder more of these household burdens than their partners do—to renegotiate for themselves, day after day, the battle between the demands of employment and family. This is a process that unfolds as a thousand cutting decisions and compromises, each of which seemingly disappoints someone, until you find yourself writing at 4:00 a.m. next to a precarious pile of laundry. In a particularly heartbreaking (and distressingly familiar) anecdote from *Overwhelmed*, Schulte's daughter complains about how much time her mom spends on the computer. She tells Schulte that when she grows up, she wants to be a teacher, explaining, "because then at least I'll be able to spend time with my kids."

Parents, of course, aren't alone in suffering under the work-life tensions produced by pseudo-productivity. If you're struggling to care for a sick relative, or dealing with an illness of your own, or grappling with any number of other disruptive life events, the demand to prove your worth through visible activity produces similar inner turmoil. A particularly widely felt example of these dynamics came from the pandemic, which acted as such a powerful accelerant to the burgeoning anti-productivity movement, in part, because of the way in which the logic of pseudo-productivity demanded knowledge workers continue their frenzied dance of electronic busyness even as Rome seemingly burned around them. What was needed was time and space to adjust and grieve. What was provided instead were upgraded Zoom accounts and cheerful email exhortations to "stay productive." It was crazy-making.

This chapter details concrete propositions to help you reduce your professional workload. These propositions, which are filled with specific strategies and suggestions, reinforce the economic pragmatism that opened our discussion of this principle. Doing less can indeed lead to more. I thought it important, however, to take a break from this otherwise sensible discussion to recognize the messier and more human side of this idea. For many, the redemption found in doing fewer things goes well beyond the professional. It's also about finding an escape hatch from a psychologically untenable relationship with your work. To be overloaded is not just inefficient; it can be, for many, downright inhumane.

This reality should motivate those in this position to energetically embrace the strategies discussed in this chapter. To avoid projects that generate excessive tasks, or to spend more money to outsource busywork, is not some sort of shady hack you hope your employer or clients don't notice. If your job, like so many in the era of pseudo-productivity, leaves it up to you to manage your own load, then you have every right to step up to this challenge with intention and determination. This first principle of slow productivity is not just about a more effective way to organize work, it also provides a response for those who feel like their work is corroding away all the other attributes of their existence.

Proposition: Pull Instead of Push

During my first years as a PhD student at MIT, I would pass, on my morning walk from the Kendall subway stop to my office, by a construction site on which a sleek glass-fronted building slowly began to rise. It was the new home of the Broad Institute, a joint venture between MIT and Harvard that had recently launched to great fanfare with a founding gift of $100 million from its benefactors, Eli and Edythe Broad. I knew vaguely that the institute was doing cutting-edge research in the emerging field of genomics. I also know it was considered a big deal. What I didn't find out until later, however, was that behind all that polished glass, many of those who worked at the Broad Institute were struggling to keep up with their tasks.

According to a case study in *MIT Sloan Management Review* titled "Breaking Logjams in Knowledge Work," the trouble started with the genetic sequencing pipeline. One of the major services offered by Broad was the ability to process samples sent in by scientists from around the world. These samples would be run through a series of stages, like stations on an assembly line, where they would be prepped for analysis in Broad's massive sequencing machines. The result of all of this chemical poking and prodding was a printout of the sample's underlying genetic code.

As the authors of the article detail, it didn't take long before this assembly line began to sputter. The technicians running each stage of the process resorted to a natural "push" strategy, in which they processed incoming samples as fast as they could, shoving them off to the next stage as soon as they were done. Not every stage, however, took the same amount of time to complete. The slower stages soon faced large backlogs of samples to be processed, which created problems. "The [backlogs] continued to grow, far exceeding any optimum level," the authors explain. "When somebody needed a specific sample, it could take two days to find it. Managing the consequent congestion and confusion occupied an increasing portion of the leadership team's time." The average time between a sample arriving and its sequence being returned increased to 120 days. Frustrated scientists began to send their samples to other laboratories.

The solution the Broad Institute came up with wasn't new, but instead an adaptation of a technique common in the world of industrial manufacturing: switching the flow of their genetic sequencing process from "push" to "pull." In a push-based process, each stage pushes work onward to the next as soon as it's done. In a pull-based process, by contrast, each stage *pulls* in new work only when it's ready for it. At Broad, this pull methodology was implemented in a simple manner. Each stage maintained a tray to place the completed samples. The next stage would pull in new samples from this same tray. If the outgoing tray at a given stage began to fill, then the technicians filling it would slow down their work. In some cases, they would even offer their assistance to the next stage to help them catch up.

Shifting to a pull-based operation made backlogs impossible: the pace of the pipeline would adapt to whatever stage was running slowest. This transparency, in turn, helped the workers identify places where the system was out of balance. "A perpetually full pull box means either the downstream task is moving too slowly or the upstream one is moving too quickly," write the authors. "An empty pull box at the end of the day means that something is wrong with the operation that feeds it." The improvements yielded by this approach were quantifiable. The usage rate of the institute's expensive sequencing machines more than doubled, while the average time to process each sample fell by more than 85 percent.

At the Broad Institute, the solution to overload in its genetic sequencing process was to switch from a push model to a pull model. Can this same solution apply to the frustrated knowledge worker overloaded by too many emails and project requests? Fascinatingly, the authors of this same *Management Review* article also provide insight into this natural follow-up question. It turns out that after witnessing the transformation of the sequencing pipeline, the technology development group at Broad, a team of IT professionals tasked with building novel digital tools to help the scientists, decided they, too, would experiment with a pull-based workflow.

As with those working on sequencing, the technology development group was also plagued by backlogs. "The group had many more ideas for tech development under consideration than it could fully investigate and many more projects under way than its overloaded operations team could ever implement," the authors explain. Any engineer could push a new idea into consideration at any time, and because the engineers were smart, they came up with lots of ideas. The system soon became bogged down by its own excessive ambition. If a project was deemed particularly vital, it would be "expedited," leaving the team to "drop everything and fight the new fire." The individual engineers found themselves frantically juggling more projects than they could handle, with new priorities constantly arriving, and demands for their attention shifting unpredictably.

To solve these issues, the group decided to change the process by which work was assigned. As with the newly improved sequencing pipeline, they wanted to transition from a system in which new tasks could be pushed onto their plate haphazardly to one in which they would pull in new work only when they were ready for it. To accomplish this goal, they sketched a diagram on some unused wall space that included a box for each step of their design process, starting with the initial idea and continuing all the way through testing and deployment. Specific projects were represented by Post-it notes stuck on the wall in the box corresponding to the current stage in this process. Each of these notes was labeled with the names of the engineers who were currently working on it, making it clear exactly what everyone was currently up to.

The full group would meet weekly to discuss the status of every Post-it stuck to the wall. If a project was ready to advance to the next stage, the team leader would need to identify engineers with enough spare capacity to take it on. Their names would be added to the note, which would then be moved to the next box. Similarly, it became easy to notice if a project was struggling, as its note would have stopped advancing. At this point, engineers with spare capacity could be added, or the decision could be made to shut down the project altogether. The key to this system is that it prevented an unbounded amount of work from being pushed onto any individual's plate. An engineer could only *pull* in new work if they had sufficient spare capacity, a status that was easy to determine by surveying how often their name came up on the wall. Overload became impossible. Not surprisingly, after switching to this more structured pull strategy, the total number of projects underway in the technology development group fell by almost 50 percent, while the rate at which projects were completed notably increased.

Inspired in part by this article, I've become convinced in recent years that pull workflows are a powerful tool to avoid overload in the knowledge work setting. If you're in a position to change the way your company or team organizes its work, moving to a pull strategy, similar to that deployed by the technology development group at the Broad Institute, can yield spectacular returns. Not only will your organization complete projects at a faster rate, your team members will revel in their newfound liberation from the scourge of having too much to do.

The situation becomes trickier, however, when we turn our attention to individuals without direct control over how their work is assigned. Perhaps you're employed by a company that still worships at the altar of a faster brand of productivity, or you're a solopreneur dealing with clients who aren't interested in learning some complicated new system. Haphazard, push-based workflows might seem unavoidable for the many who are stuck in such settings, but they don't have to be. It's possible to reap a substantial fraction of the advantages of a more enlightened pull approach even when you lack full control over your work environment. The key is to *simulate* a pull-based assignment system in such a way that the people you work with don't even realize you're trying something new.

What follows is a three-strep strategy for implementing a simulated pull system as an individual without control over the habits of your colleagues or clients. Such an individualized system, of course, is not as effective as having everyone on the same page about abandoning pushes, but it's still much better than the default response of throwing up your hands and letting work be flung toward you from all directions, sighing in frustration as your metaphorical tray of samples begins to overflow.

SIMULATED PULL, PART 1: HOLDING TANK AND ACTIVE LISTS

The first step in simulating a pull-based workflow is tracking all projects to which you're currently committed on a list divided into two sections: "holding tank" and "active." (The format used for storing this list doesn't really matter. You can use a text file on your computer, for example, or an old-fashioned notebook: whatever you find easiest.) Recall, when I say "projects," I mean something substantial enough to require multiple sessions to complete. (Strategies for containing smaller commitments, which we call "tasks," were discussed in the preceding proposition.) When a new project is pushed toward you, place it in the holding-pen section of your list. There is no bound to the size of your holding tank.

The active position of the list, by contrast, should be limited to three projects at most. When scheduling your time, you should focus your attention only on the projects on your active list. When you complete one of these projects, you can remove it from your list. This leaves open a free slot that you can fill by *pulling* in a new project from the holding tank. For larger projects, you might want to instead pull onto your active list a reasonable chunk of work toward its completion. For example, if "write book" is in your holding tank, and a free slot opens up on your active list, you might pull in "write next chapter of book" to work on next. In this case, the larger project, "write book," would remain in the holding tank until completely finished.

In maintaining these two lists, you're simulating the core dynamic of a pull-based workflow. The number of things on which you're actively working is limited to a fixed, small quantity, freeing you from a sense of frenzied overload and minimizing the overhead tax discussed earlier in this chapter. The problem, of course, is that the colleagues or clients pushing projects toward you don't know about your fancy simulated system, and might get frustrated at your visible lack of progress on their demands. To avoid a barrage of incessant prodding, you need to combine your lists with a smart intake procedure. This is the step we'll discuss next.

SIMULATED PULL, PART 2: INTAKE PROCEDURE

When adding a new project to your holding tank, it's important to update the source of this new obligation about what they should expect. To do so, send an *acknowledgment message* that formally acknowledges the project that you're committing to complete, but that also includes the following three pieces of extra information: (1) a request for any additional details you need from the source before you can start the project, (2) a count of the number of existing projects already on your lists, and (3) an estimate of when you expect to complete this new work.

After sending this message, label the project with the time estimate you included in your acknowledgment message so you won't later forget. Notice, when making this estimate, you can look at the estimates on all of your existing projects to help inform a realistic prediction.

Here's an example of an acknowledgment message:

> Hi, Hasini,
>
> I wanted to follow up on our conversation from earlier this morning and confirm that I'll take charge of updating the client section of our website. What I'll need from you before getting started is a list of what elements you think the new section needs (or a link to another company's site that you think does it right). At the moment, I have eleven other projects queued up ahead of

> this. Based on my commitments to these existing projects, my best guess is that I'll be able to get to this in roughly four weeks after I get the needed information from you. I will, of course, update you if this estimate changes.
>
> *— Cal*

If you fall behind on a project, update your estimate and inform the person who originally sent you the work about the delay. The key here is transparency. Be clear about what's going on, and deliver on your promises, even if these promises have to change. Never let a project just drop through the cracks and hope it will be forgotten. If your colleagues and clients don't trust you to deliver, they won't stop bothering you. This observation is important if you want to succeed with this method. We often believe those we work with care only about getting results as fast as possible. But this isn't true. Often what they really want is the ability to hand something off and not have to worry about whether or not it will be accomplished. If they trust you, they'll give you latitude to finish things on your own terms. Relief, in other words, trumps expediency.

A secondary benefit of a good intake procedure is that it often leads people to withdraw their requests. It's common, for example, for a boss to shoot off an idea to an employee on a whim. When this request gets formalized, however, and the boss sees that they need to provide you with more information, and they're confronted with the reality of your current workload, they might simply respond, "On second thought, let's put a pin in this one for now." Sometimes, a little friction is all it takes to slow down a torrent of incoming work.

SIMULATED PULL, PART 3: LIST CLEANING

You should update and clean your lists once a week. In addition to pulling in new work to fill empty slots on your active list, you should also review upcoming deadlines. Prioritize what's due soon, and send updates for any work that you know you're not going to finish by the time promised. These cleaning sessions also provide a good opportunity to remove from your holding tank projects that are languishing. If you've delayed the same project again and again, for example, this might be a good sign that you're not really equipped to handle it, or that it falls outside your comfort zone.

In these cases, consider just bluntly asking the original source of the project to release you from your obligation:

> *I know I said I would work on the new client section of our website, but I've found myself, as you've undoubtedly noticed, delaying this work again and again. I think this is a sign that I don't really know enough about what we're trying to accomplish here to make progress. Unless you object, I would like to take this off my list for now. I think we probably need to engage help from the web development team to make real progress on this goal.*

Finally, when cleaning your lists, look for projects that have become redundant or have been rendered obsolete by subsequent developments. That client web page you're supposed to update, for example, might no longer be relevant after your boss decides to hire a company to redesign the entire corporate web presence from scratch. In these cases, remove the outdated projects from your lists. But before you do so, send a quick note to their original source letting them know. Simulating a pull-based workflow works only if you maintain transparency.

4 | WORK AT A NATURAL PACE

The Second Principle of Slow Productivity

The insight came all at once. It was the summer of 2021, and I was on vacation in Maine, sitting outside our small rental house on the harbor at York. I was reading John Gribbin's monumental 2002 history, *The Scientists*, which presents capsule biographies of the great theorists and experimentalists who created the modern scientific enterprise. What struck me as I read were two contradictory observations that seemed to be true at the same time. These great scientists of times past were clearly "productive" by any reasonable definition of the term. What else can you call it when someone literally changes our understanding of the universe? At the same time, however, the *pace* at which they toiled on their momentous discoveries seemed, by modern standards, to be uneven, and in some cases almost leisurely.

Copernicus's revolutionary ideas about planetary motion, for example, were sparked by a new commentary on Ptolemy published in 1496, which the young astronomer read when he was twenty-three years old. It wasn't until 1510, however, that Copernicus got around to writing down his theories in a working draft that he passed around to friends. It then took another three decades before he finally published his masterwork, *On the Revolutions of the Celestial Spheres*, for a broader audience. Tycho Brahe, whose careful astronomical data collection would lay the foundation for the eventual acceptances of Copernicus's theories, wasn't any faster in his work. His classic observations on the bright comet that crossed the night skies of Europe in 1577 weren't fully analyzed and published until 1588.

The emergence of physics was similarly languid. Galileo famously used his pulse to time swinging chandeliers in the Cathedral of Pisa in either 1584 or 1585. But he didn't get around to conducting his follow-up experiments, which led to the identification of the laws of pendulum motion, until 1602. Isaac Newton began thinking seriously about gravity in the summer of 1655, after he fled the plague in Cambridge for the quiet countryside of Lincolnshire. It took him until 1670 before he felt he really had a handle on the inverse square law, and then another fifteen years or so before he finally publicized his paradigm-shifting theories.*

---

* As John Gribbin points out, Newton, later in his life, publicized the story of the apple falling from the tree as a way to place his discovery of the inverse square law of gravitation all the way back to that initial visit to Lincolnshire in 1655. This was marketing. His writings from the period make it clear that these ideas emerged more gradually over a period of multiple years *starting* in 1655. For more, see John Gribbin, *The Scientists: A History of Science Told through the Lives of Its Greatest Inventors* (New York: Random House Trade Paperbacks, 2004), 185–86.

This unhurried pace was not restricted to the men of the Renaissance. If we jump ahead to the summer of 1896, we find Marie Curie deep into a series of experiments involving the *radioactivity*—a new term she had recently coined—of a substance called pitchblende. Curie was convinced that pitchblende contained a new, fiercely active element that had not yet been identified by science. This was a big deal. To isolate and describe a new element of this type would be a career-defining, Nobel Prize–worthy discovery. It was at exactly this moment, at the precipice of potential, that Marie, along with her husband Pierre and newborn baby daughter, decided to shutter their modest flat in Paris and retreat into the French countryside for an extended vacation, where, according to the biography written by their daughter Eve, "they climbed hills, visited grottoes, bathed in rivers."

While still up in Maine that summer, I wrote a short essay about these observations that I titled "On Pace and Productivity." In this piece, I observed that when it comes to our understanding of productivity, *timescale matters*. When viewed at the fast scale of days and weeks, the efforts of historic thinkers like Copernicus and Newton can seem uneven and delayed. When instead viewed at the slow scale of years, their efforts suddenly seem undeniably and impressively fruitful. Her 1896 countryside vacation was far from her mind when Marie Curie took the stage in Stockholm seven years later to receive her first of two Nobel Prizes.

In the time that's passed since that original insight formed in Maine, I've elaborated my theories on the ways that pace affects our experience of our professional efforts. In contemporary work, it became clear, our bias is toward evaluating our efforts at the fast scale. This isn't surprising. As I argued in the first part of this book, when knowledge work emerged as a major economic sector in the twentieth century, we reacted to the shock of all this newness by adapting hurried, industrial notions of productivity. As John Gribbin reminds us, however, this isn't the only way to think about pacing work.

The great scientists of past eras would have found our urgency to be self-defeating and frantic. They were interested in what they produced over the course of their lifetimes, not in any particular short-term stretch. Without a manager looking over their shoulder, or clients pestering them about responding to emails, they didn't feel pressure to be maximally busy every day. They were instead comfortable taking longer on projects and adopting a more forgiving and variable rhythm to their work. Curie wasn't unique in her decision to retreat for a summer of reflection and recharging. Galileo enjoyed visits to a villa owned by his friends in the countryside near Padua. Once there, he would take long walks in the hills and enjoy sleeping in a room ingeniously air-conditioned by a series of ducts that carried in cool air from a nearby cave system.* And Newton, of course, made much of his extended visits to Lincolnshire, home to the famed apple tree.

Above all else, these scientists tended to adopt a perspective on

---

* This system was far from perfect. As Gribbin notes, during one unfortunate evening, noxious gases from the cave system, fed through the ducts, caused Galileo and his two companions in the room to suffer a grave illness that killed one of them and afflicted Galileo for the rest of his life. Gribbin, *The Scientists*, 80.

their professional efforts that was more philosophical than instrumental. In the *Nicomachean Ethics*, which would have been familiar to any serious thinker from the time of Copernicus onward, Aristotle identified deep contemplation as the most human and worthy of all activities. The general lifestyle of the scientist, by this logic, had a worthiness of its own, independent of any specific accomplishments in the moment. Little value was to be gained in rushing, as the work itself provided reward. This mindset supported a Renaissance-style understanding of professional efforts as one element among many that combine to create a flourishing existence. "Alongside all this, Galileo had a full private life," writes Gribbin. "He studied literature and poetry, attended the theatre regularly and continued to play the lute to a high standard."

The second principle of slow productivity argues that these famous scientists were onto something. Our exhausting tendency to grind without relief, hour after hour, day after day, month after month, is more arbitrary than we recognize. It's true that many of us have bosses or clients making demands, but they don't always dictate the details of our daily schedules—it's often our own anxieties that play the role of the fiercest taskmaster. We suffer from overly ambitious timelines and poorly managed workloads due to a fundamental uneasiness with ever stepping back from the numbing exhaustion of jittery busyness.

These scientists point toward an alternative approach to scheduling work in which we give our important efforts more breathing room, allowing them to take longer and unfold with intensity levels that vary over time. This approach is not only more sustainable and humane, it's also arguably the better long-term strategy for producing results that matter. In the sixteenth century, Galileo's professional life was more leisurely and less intense than that of the average twenty-first-century knowledge worker. Yet he still managed to change the course of human intellectual history.

We can condense these ideas into a pragmatic principle as follows:

PRINCIPLE #2: WORK AT A NATURAL PACE

Don't rush your most important work. Allow it instead to unfold along a sustainable timeline, with variations in intensity, in settings conducive to brilliance.

In the sections that follow, I'll start by expanding my arguments in favor of working at a calmer speed. There's a reason, it will turn out, why all of these scientists converged on the same, more considered approach to their efforts: it's much more natural than the homogenized busyness that defines the modern workday. I'll then move into a series of propositions about how to specifically implement this second principle in your own professional life. It's here that we'll dive into the details of clever timeline heuristics and simulated quiet seasons. More important than these specific suggestions, however, is the broader message captured by this chapter. Slow productivity emphatically rejects the performative rewards of unwavering urgency. There will always be more work to do. You should give your efforts the breathing room and respect required to make them part of a life well lived, not an obstacle to it.

From Foraging to the Invisible Factory; or, Why Knowledge Workers Should Return to a More Natural Pace

In the fall of 1963, an enterprising young anthropologist named Richard Lee journeyed to the Dobe region of the northwest Kalahari Desert, in southern Africa. He was there to live among a community known as the Ju/'hoansi, which was made up of approximately four hundred and sixty individuals, split among fourteen independent camps. This area of the Kalahari was semiarid and suffered from drought every two or three years, leading Lee to describe it as "a marginal environment for human habitation." The demanding conditions made the territory of the Ju/'hoansi less desirable to farmers and herders, allowing the community to live in relative isolation well into the twentieth century.

As Lee would later explain, the Ju/'hoansi were not completely cut off from the world. When he arrived, for example, they were trading with nearby Tswana cattle herders and encountered Europeans on colonial patrols. But the lack of extensive contact with the local economy meant that the Ju/'hoansi still relied primarily on hunting and gathering for their sustenance. It was commonly believed at the time that acquiring food without the stability and abundance of agriculture was perilous and grueling. Lee wanted to find out whether this was true.

Humans in more or less our current modern form have walked the earth for roughly three hundred thousand years. For all but the last ten thousand or so of these many years, we lived as seminomadic hunters and gatherers. These timescales are sufficiently vast for the insistent logics of natural selection to adapt our bodies and brains toward an existence in which our experience of "work" was centered on foraging. When seeking to understand the friction points in contemporary office life, therefore, a good place to start might be to identify where our current work routines most differ from what our prehistoric ancestors evolved to expect.

The problem with this approach, of course, is that there are no prehistoric humans left, and archaeological digs reveal only fragmentary glimpses into the realities of this past era. Fortunately, modern anthropology, building off the pioneering work of Richard Lee, identified a partial solution to this issue: study, with care, the dwindling number of existing communities that still rely largely on hunting and gathering for their sustenance. As researchers like Lee are quick to emphasize, these extant foraging groups are *not* left over from an ancient age, but are instead modern individuals living in, and connected to, the modern world. But what we can learn from these examples is a fuller understanding of the daily realities of hunting and gathering as a primary means of survival, providing a more detailed look, in other words, at what "work" meant for most of human existence.

After fifteen months of field research, extending from the fall of 1963 into the early winter of 1965, Lee was ready to present his results to the world. Working with his longtime collaborator Irven DeVore, he organized a splashy conference in Chicago the following spring. It was called "Man the Hunter," and it promised to provide anthropology with its "first intensive survey of a single, crucial stage of human development—man's once universal hunting way of life." The clamor around the event was such that the eminent French anthropologist Claude Lévi-Strauss traveled to America to attend.

Lee stole the show with a paper that described the results of his time spent among the Ju/'hoansi. It opens by repeating the common assumption that hunter-gatherer life is "generally a precarious and arduous struggle for existence," then methodically presents data to undermine that idea. The community that Lee studied turned out to be well fed, consuming more than two thousand calories a day, even during a historic drought in Botswana. Equally striking was the observation that the Ju/'hoansi appeared to work less than the farmers around them. According to Lee's data, the adults he studied spent, on average, around twenty hours a week acquiring food, with an additional twenty hours or so dedicated to other chores—providing abundant leisure time.

As Lee summarizes, much can be guessed about our species' ancient relationship with work from these modern observations:

The Dobe-area Bushmen live well today on wild plants and meat, in spite of the fact that they are confined to the least productive portion of the range in which Bushman peoples were formerly found. It is likely that an even more substantial subsistence base would have been characteristic of these hunters and gatherers in the past.

As would be expected, this early study of hunting and gathering lifestyles underwent a fair amount of later criticism. Lee's time-diary data-gathering method was perhaps too inaccurate, for example, and there was debate about whether he was correctly coding all relevant activities as "work." His big idea, however, that we can learn about ancient economies by studying modern foraging communities, proved immensely influential.

We can find a more refined snapshot of the type of data that Lee set out to gather in the much more recent work of a research team lead by Mark Dyble, currently an assistant professor of evolutionary anthropology at the University of Cambridge. As reported in a landmark 2019 paper appearing in the journal *Nature Human Behaviour*, Dyble and his team aimed to replicate Lee's general study, but now using updated methods. They observed the Agta of the northern Philippines, a community well suited for the comparison of different models of food acquisition, as some of them still largely depended on hunting and gathering, while others had recently shifted toward rice farming. Both groups shared the same culture and environment, allowing a cleaner comparison between the two food-acquisition strategies. Dyble's team diverged from the diary approach used by Lee, in which the researcher attempts to capture all the activities of their subjects' day (which turns out to be quite hard), and instead deployed the more modern experience-sampling method, in which, at randomly generated intervals, the researchers record what their subjects are doing at that exact moment. The goal was to calculate, for both the farmers and the foragers, the relative proportion of samples dedicated to leisure versus work activities.

"The group engaged entirely in foraging spent forty to fifty per cent of daylight hours at leisure," Dyble told me, when I asked him to summarize his team's results, "versus more like thirty per cent for those who engage entirely in farming." His data validates Lee's claim that hunter-gatherers enjoy more leisure time than agriculturalists, though perhaps not to the same extreme as what was originally reported. Missing from these high-level numbers, however, is an equally important observation: how this leisure time was *distributed* throughout the day. As Dyble explained, while the farmers engaged in "monotonous, continuous work," the pace of the foragers' schedules was more varied, with long respites interspersed throughout their daily efforts. "Hunting trips required a long hike through the forest, so you'd be out all day, but you'd have breaks," Dyble told me. "With something like fishing, there are spikes, ups and downs . . . only a small per cent of their time is spent actually fishing."

For our purposes, the key observation from Dyble's study is the uneven nature of the foragers' efforts. A busy start to a fishing expedition might also involve a long nap in the boat during the midday doldrums. An exhausting hunting trip might be followed by multiple days waiting out the rain, doing very little. The rice-farming Agta, by contrast, worked continuously, sunrise to sunset, when planting or harvesting. Compared with the activities of their foraging brethren, these farming efforts struck Dyble as "monotonous." This side-by-side comparison underscores the degree to which our experience of work has transformed during the recent past of our species. Our shift from hunting and gathering to agriculture—the Neolithic Revolution—only really picked up speed somewhere around twelve thousand years ago. By the time of the Roman Empire, foraging had almost completely disappeared from the human story. This reorientation toward agriculture threw most of humanity into a state similar to that of the rice-farming Agta, grappling with something new: the continuous monotony of unvarying work, all day long, day after day.

The one saving grace in this scenario is that agriculture didn't demand this homogenized effort the entire year, as the busy sowing and gathering of crops is offset by the quiet of winter. Humanity soon developed rituals to structure and make sense of these on-and-off rhythms. Harvest festivals encouraged the intense work required each fall to bring in the crops, while elaborate winter celebrations helped add meaning to the idleness of the dark months that followed. For the ancient Germanic peoples, for example, the multiday feasts surrounding Yule, replete with animal sacrifices and the veneration of the dead around bright-burning fires, transformed the shortest days of the year into something more than a hardship to endure.

The Industrial Revolution stripped away those last vestiges of variation in our work efforts. The powered mill, followed by the factory, made every day a harvest day—continuous, monotonous labor that never alters. Gone were the seasonal changes and sense-making rituals. Marx, for all his flaws and overreach, hit on something deep with his theory of *Entfremdung* (estrangement), which argued that the industrial order alienated us from our basic human nature. The workers eventually—inevitably—fought back against this grim situation. They pushed for reform legislation, like the Fair Labor Standards Act (passed by the US Congress in 1938), which fixed forty hours as the standard workweek, limiting the fraction of the day that could be snared in monotonous effort without extra pay. They also formed labor unions as a counterbalance to the more dehumanizing aspects of industrialization. If we were going to lock our days into activities that alienated us from our basic nature, we wanted (to the extent possible) to make sure we were doing so on our own terms.

Then knowledge work entered the scene as a major economic sector. As discussed in part 1, the managerial class didn't know how to handle the autonomy and variety of jobs in this new sector. Their stopgap response was pseudo-productivity, which used visible activity as a proxy for usefulness. Under this new configuration, we took another step backward. As in the industrial sector, we continued to work all day, every day, without seasonal changes, as any such variation would now be received as nonproductiveness. But unlike in the industrial sector, in this *invisible factory* we'd constructed for ourselves we didn't have reform legislation or unions to identify the most draining aspects of this setup and fight for limits. Knowledge work was free to totalize our existence: colonizing as much of our time, from evenings to weekends to vacations, as we could bear, and leaving little recourse beyond burnout or demotion or quitting when it became too much. Our estrangement from the rhythms of work that dominated the first two hundred eighty thousand years of our species' existence was now complete.

Lurking behind this exhaustion, however, are glimpses of a better future. Monotonous, all-day effort is unavoidable when you're harvesting crops or working an assembly-line station—the best you can do is mitigate its worst impacts with rituals and laws. It's less clear that this unvarying intensity is equally as unavoidable in knowledge work. We toil long days, every day, to satisfy the demands of pseudo-productivity, not because skilled cognitive efforts actually require such unwavering attention. If anything, we have evidence to believe that industrial-style work rhythms make us *less* effective. Recall that the scientists with whom we opened this chapter leveraged the freedom of their rarefied positions to implement an up-and-down pace that more closely resembled an Agta forager than a modern office dweller. Freed to work in any way they wanted, these traditional knowledge workers—not surprisingly—returned to the more varied effort levels for which humans are wired.

It's here that we find the justification for the second principle of slow productivity. Working with unceasing intensity is artificial and unsustainable. In the moment, it might exude a false sense of usefulness, but when continued over time, it estranges us from our fundamental nature, generates misery, and, from a strictly economic perspective, almost certainly holds us back from reaching our full capabilities. A more natural, slower, varied pace to work is the foundation of true productivity in the long term. What follows is a collection of propositions about how you can inject such variation into your current professional situation. Most of us don't share Marie Curie's ability to set off on multi-month vacations to clear our minds, but if you're careful about how you leverage the autonomy and ambiguity intertwined into most modern knowledge sector jobs, you might be surprised by the degree to which you do have the power to transform the pace of your work into something much more, for lack of a better word, human.

Proposition: Take Longer

Lin-Manuel Miranda wrote the first draft of *In the Heights* during his sophomore year at Wesleyan University. He staged the first performance of the show, which would eventually go on to win multiple Tony Awards, in a campus theater during the spring of 2000. He was only twenty years old. This story of immense precociousness has become part of the Miranda lore, where it provides the initial revelation of a generational talent. What's often left out of this narrative, however, is what happened between that initial performance and the show's triumphant Broadway debut eight years later.

The one-act musical Miranda presented in 2000 was far different from the nearly two-and-a-half-hour-long showcase of exuberant music and choreography that eventually opened at the Richard Rodgers Theatre. As Rebecca Mead notes in her classic 2015 *New*

Yorker profile of Miranda, the undergraduate version of *In the Heights* was "shopworn," focusing on a cliché love triangle storyline. The twenty-year-old's play wasn't received with enthusiasm by his peers. As Miranda later revealed in an interview with Marc Maron, the culture at Wesleyan focused more on experimental drama. His interest in classical musical productions put him at odds with his classmates. "Trying to make musical theater happen was very hard at Wesleyan," he said. Miranda put his hip-hop musical aside, turning his attention instead to his senior project, an ultimately forgettable production called *On Borrowed Time*. After graduating, Miranda took a job as a substitute teacher. His father urged him to apply to law school.

Not everyone, however, dismissed *In the Heights*. The lukewarm writing was what you might expect from a college sophomore, but the score was special. "This mix of Latin music and hip-hop was potent," Miranda recalled. "There was something in that groove." Thomas Kail, who was two years ahead of Miranda at Wesleyan, remembered *In the Heights*. Soon after Miranda graduated, they met to discuss the play's potential. Miranda began working with Kail on improving the music and the book, with Kail informally taking on the role of director for the embryonic show. This duo soon connected with two other Wesleyan graduates, John Buffalo Mailer and Neil Stewart, who had cofounded a theater company in New York City called Back House Productions. They began staging readings of Miranda's evolving work in progress.

The rapid feedback loop created by these repeated mini-performances helped Miranda find his signature musical voice. The writing, however, still felt flat. To solve this problem, Miranda and

Kail brought onto the project a talented young playwright named Quiara Alegría Hudes, who would go on to win a Pulitzer Prize in 2012. In the fall of 2004, they submitted *In the Heights* to the National Music Theater Conference, a program, run out of the Eugene O'Neill Theater Center in Waterford, Connecticut, designed to help incubate new musical theater productions. Their play was selected, and the group, now joined by music director Alex Lacamoire, moved to Connecticut to work full time on crafting a more developed production.

This is when things began to come together for *In the Heights*. Hudes simplified the character storylines, shifting emphasis to the musical celebration of the Washington Heights neighborhood in which the play was set. "It was clear after seeing it at the O'Neill that the neighborhood was the central love story," explained Kail. This showcase in Connecticut attracted the attention of serious Broadway producers, and with it real financial support. But considerable work remained until the show would be ready for paying audiences. It wasn't until 2007—a half decade after Miranda began working seriously with Kail on the play, and seven years since it was first performed at Wesleyan—that *In the Heights* made its debut on a professional stage. It would be yet another year before it would move to Broadway and Miranda would win his Tony Awards.*

---

* A few months after these triumphs, Miranda would find himself lounging in a pool on a much-needed vacation in Mexico, failing to find relaxation because his attention had been captured by a doorstop of a book he had impulsively purchased before his trip. It was a biography of Alexander Hamilton.

In Lin-Manuel Miranda's story we find a clear example of one of the general patterns we identified earlier in the lives of the great scientists: he took his time. He allowed the creative development of his play to unfold slowly in the seven years that followed its initial performance. There were certainly many stretches during this period when Miranda was giving *In the Heights* his full laser focus. But there were also many stretches in which he was engaged with other pursuits. During these years, in addition to his substitute teaching job, Miranda wrote a column and restaurant reviews for the *Manhattan Times*. He also toured internationally with an improv comedy and rap crew he founded called Freestyle Love Supreme, and helped Stephen Sondheim, whom Miranda had met at Wesleyan, translate lyrics into Spanish for a Broadway revival of *West Side Story*.

The pseudo-productivity mindset is uncomfortable with spreading out work on an important project, as time not spent hammering on your most important goals seems like time wasted. To a true believer in this fast philosophy, watching Miranda in the early 2000s burn energy freestyle rapping with Freestyle Love Supreme, or writing columns for a small newspaper, might have been frustrating—a tableau of a great talent diluted. The slow productivity mindset, by contrast, finds advantages to a more languid pace. Frequent cold starts can inject more creativity into your efforts, an effect Miranda seems to have leveraged in the uneven but insistent improvement of *In the Heights*. It also allowed him to explore and develop as both a creative and a human being. College sophomore Miranda wasn't confident, experienced, or interesting enough to produce a Broadway-caliber version of his show. His greatness needed to take its time before it could fully emerge.

The second principle of slow productivity asks that you approach your work with a more natural pace. This proposition offers the first of three ideas for how to achieve this goal: follow Lin-Manuel Miranda's lead and become comfortable taking longer on important projects. This request, of course, is fraught. The boundary between Miranda's slow but steady creative production and straight-up procrastination is worrisomely narrow. There's a reason why the frenetic speed of National Novel Writing Month is so popular—many people don't trust themselves to keep returning to a hard project once their initial ardor dissipates. The collection of concrete advice that follows is designed to compensate for these fears. It will provide structure to your attempts to take longer, allowing you to preserve your drive to produce things that matter while avoiding the frantic sense of there always being more you need to do right now.

MAKE A FIVE-YEAR PLAN

Most people restrict their long-term planning to cover something like the next few months. You might have a goal, for example, to write and submit an academic paper by the end of the fall, or introduce a new product over the summer. Planning at this scale is certainly necessary, as without it you might end up mired in shallow demands and never really move forward on anything important. I suggest, however, also crafting a plan that covers an even larger scale: what you would like to accomplish in the next five years or so. The specific choice of five years is somewhat arbitrary. You can adjust this quantity to fit the reality of your situation: if you've just started a four-year degree program, for example, a four-year plan might make more sense. The key to this suggestion, however, is that your time horizon should include at least several years.

To make this more tangible, I'll use myself as case study. When I started the computer science doctoral program at MIT, I had just submitted the manuscript for my first book to Random House. I knew I wanted to be a writer in addition to my academic career, but I also knew that the immediate pressures of MIT would, if unchecked, push me away from this goal. In response, I detailed a vision of how I wanted the next half decade to unfold. I would, I decided, find a way to keep publishing books while a graduate student. I wanted to leave MIT as an established author with multiple titles to my name, even if this would require periods of stress and uncertainty along the way.

This long-term plan kept me returning to my writing goals time and again. But equally important, it gave me the breathing room I needed to feel comfortable even when progress wasn't immediately being made. Because my vision was established on the scale of multiple years, I could tolerate busy periods in which academic demands left little room for writing. I could also tolerate extended interludes between books, during which I questioned what I wanted to write next. During the four-year gap between my second and third books, for example, I experimented with new styles, both on my blog and in freelance writing assignments. I was slowly and carefully trying to lay the foundation for making a move from writing student advice guides, where I was successful, to penning more serious idea books, where I had no presence. My long-term plan enabled me to embrace this slower development as a writer. I could explore without feeling like I had given up. I wanted to write multiple books before I graduated, but there were many winding paths that would deliver me to this destination.

The idea that adding *more* plans to your life can help you slow down might seem paradoxical. The magic here is in the way that this strategy expands the timescales at which you're evaluating your productivity. Lin-Manuel Miranda didn't toil continuously on *In the Heights* during the years immediately following his graduation from Wesleyan, but he did keep returning to it, again and again, until it developed into something remarkable. This slow but steady pace was only possible in the context of long-term vision.

DOUBLE YOUR PROJECT TIMELINES

We move now from multiyear plans to rethinking how you organize your work for the next few months. At this seasonal scale, you're typically planning either complete projects, such as launching a new web site, or milestones from larger pursuits, such as completing the first three chapters of a book. Your goals at this scale have a significant impact on the speed of your work. If you're too ambitious, your intensity will remain pegged at a high level as you scramble to try to hit your targets. If you instead give yourself more than enough time to accomplish your objectives, the pace of your work can fall into a more natural groove. A simple heuristic to achieve this latter state is the following: take whatever timelines you first identify as reasonable for upcoming projects, and then *double* their length. For example, if your initial instinct is to plan for spending two weeks on launching a new website, revise this goal to give yourself a full month. Similarly, if you think it's reasonable to write four book chapters between September and December, change this plan to require that you complete only two.

A reality of personal productivity is that humans are not great at estimating the time required for cognitive endeavors. We're wired to understand the demands of tangible efforts, like crafting a hand ax, or gathering edible plants. When it comes to planning pursuits for which we lack physical intuition, however, we're guessing more than we realize, leading us to gravitate toward best-case scenarios for how long things might take. We seem to seek the thrill that comes from imagining a wildly ambitious timeline during our planning: "Wow, if I could finish four chapters this fall, I'd really be ahead of schedule!" It feels good in the moment but sets us up for scrambling and disappointment in the days that follow.

By deploying a blanket policy of doubling these initial estimates, you can counter this instinct toward unjustified optimism. The result: plans that can be completed at a more leisurely pace. The fear here, of course, is that by doubling these timelines, you'll drastically reduce what you accomplish. But your original plans were never realistic or sustainable in the first place. A key tenet of slow productivity is that grand achievement is built on the steady accumulation of modest results over time. This path is long. Pace yourself.

SIMPLIFY YOUR WORKDAY

We arrive, finally, at the smallest timescale relevant to our discussion of taking longer: the individual day. One of the central joys of slowing down your work pace is that it frees you from needing to attack every day with frantic intensity. To reap this benefit, however, you actually have to simplify your daily schedule. Toning down your seasonal and long-term plans won't help if you persist in filling every hour of the current day with more work than you can hope to complete. All three timescales must be tamed together. To create more reasonable workdays, I have two suggestions: first, reduce the number of tasks you schedule, and second, reduce the number of appointments on your calendar. In other words, cut back on what you plan to accomplish while increasing your available time.

The first suggestion is simple to implement: apply the heuristic of reducing whatever task list you come up with for a given day by somewhere between 25 and 50 percent. As mentioned, humans are wildly optimistic when we estimate how much time is needed to complete cognitive efforts. Blanket reduction rules, like cutting your initial task list by a quarter, counteract this bias. When it comes to taming appointments, a good target is to ensure that no more than half of the hours in any single day are dedicated to meetings or calls. The simplest way to meet this mark is to declare certain hours to be protected (e.g., no meetings before noon). In some office contexts, of course, it might be hard to get away with strict rules of this type. ("What do you mean you don't take meetings before noon? That's when I'm available!") A subtler alternative is to instead implement a "one for you, one for me" strategy. Every time you add a meeting to your calendar for a given day, find an equal amount of time that day to protect. If I schedule thirty minutes for a call on Tuesday, I'll also find another thirty minutes that day to block off on my calendar as protected for myself. As a given day starts to fill up with appointments, it also fills up with protected blocks, making it increasingly harder to add something new. No day can end up with more than half of its time dedicated to meetings or calls. At the same time, however, this approach is more flexible than simply declaring certain hours to be always off limits. As a result, you won't seem so obviously intransigent to your colleagues.

These strategies, of course, aren't meant to apply to every day without exception. An idea we'll explore later in this chapter is that working at a natural pace will still include periods of intense busyness and effort. There will be days, in other words, where you have to go from one meeting to another, again and again, because you're trying to finalize an important deal, or get your arms around an unexpected crisis. There might also be days when every minute needs to be filled with last-minute tasks. But by thinking about these daily scheduling heuristics as a default approach to be deployed whenever possible, you ensure that unavoidable peaks in intensity will be followed by more leisurely troughs.

In her profile of Lin-Manuel Miranda, Rebecca Mead talks about his "haunted air" and "eyes ringed with fatigue" in the weeks leading up to the off-Broadway debut of *Hamilton*. She also discusses, however, the period before these final preparations, when Miranda was still composing many of the show's musical numbers. Mead described how Miranda would take long, aimless walks with his dog through the streets of New York City, listening to backing music for a new song on a loop in his headphones, waiting for melodic inspiration to strike. A period during which Miranda was taking his time.

FORGIVE YOURSELF

An important coda to this discussion about taking longer is to acknowledge its psychological perils. Timing work is tricky. Especially when it comes to complicated projects. Sometimes you might let something drag on too long: you miss deadlines or opportunities; you realize you've fallen behind on your vision; you imagined you were Lin-Manuel Miranda slowly cultivating a masterpiece, but then one day realize you've actually just been procrastinating. It's tempting to react to these periods of depressed productivity by assigning yourself a penance of crushing busyness. If you're exhausted, you tell yourself, you can't be accused of laziness.

I want to push back on this reaction. Not only is it unsustainable, but it won't, in the long run, get you any closer to producing work that matters. It's okay if your efforts to take longer sometimes temporarily lead you off your chosen path. It happens to everyone who has ever tried to accomplish something important. Even, on occasion, to Lin-Manuel Miranda. (We know about his grand successes, but we hear less about what I can only imagine to be an extensive portfolio of projects that he started in a pique of creative energy that then eventually faded.) This aspect of working at a natural pace is hard to get right, and you will be disappointed from time to time. But the humane response to this reality is obvious: Forgive yourself. Then ask, "What's next?" The key to meaningful work is in the decision to keep returning to the efforts you find important. Not in getting everything right every time.

Proposition: Embrace Seasonality

Georgia O'Keeffe's professional life got off to a busy start. In 1908, at the age of twenty-one, having studied with award-winning success at both the Art Institute of Chicago and the Art Students League in New York City, O'Keeffe ran out of money, leading her to take a job in Chicago as a commercial artist. In 1910, she moved with her family to Virginia, where she began teaching art at multiple institutions. Between 1912 and 1914, she went west, teaching art in public schools in the dusty Texas Panhandle town of Amarillo. During the summers, she returned east to act as a teaching assistant at Columbia University's Teachers College, while also taking courses at the University of Virginia. By 1915 she had an instructor role at Columbia College in South Carolina. Then she was back in New York at Teachers College. In 1916 she became the chair of the art department at West Texas State Normal College, in Canyon, Texas.

Even just listing O'Keeffe's résumé during this period is tiring. Living it must have been downright exhausting. Somehow throughout these years of hustle, O'Keeffe managed, off and on, to keep studying and developing her emerging abstract artistic style, but these efforts weren't easy. She would take long breaks from art, including one early in her career that lasted nearly four years. It was clear that something about this overloaded lifestyle would need to change before O'Keeffe could unlock her staggering artistic potential. Fortunately, in 1918, that change finally came in the form of a rambling rural property, located in the southern tip of the Adirondacks, on the western shore of Lake George.

The land was owned by the family of Alfred Stieglitz, an acclaimed photographer and the owner of the influential 291 gallery in New York City. Stieglitz came to know O'Keeffe after exhibiting a collection of her innovative charcoal works at his gallery. A friendship began that would eventually transform into a romance and, finally, marriage. Stieglitz's family had purchased their estate on Lake George, which they called Oaklawn, in the 1880s. Alfred grew up spending summers at Oaklawn. "The lake is perhaps my oldest friend," he once wrote. "Gosh! What days & nights we've had together. Calm beautiful hours. Mad static ones.—Dream hours.—Hours & days of quiet wonder."

Stieglitz was excited to introduce O'Keeffe to these "days of quiet wonder." Starting in 1918, he began bringing her to his family's estate during the summer. The first two years they stayed in the property's stately mansion, but after the Stieglitz family sold that parcel, they relocated to a humbler farmhouse, situated on a nearby hilltop. It's here that O'Keeffe found the space to fully activate her creativity. She developed a pastoral routine, where she would walk each morning into Lake George Village for her mail. Sometimes she would extend these walks by hiking the two-mile trail to Prospect Mountain, where she would be rewarded with a sweeping view of the steamers working up and down the long lake.

More than anything else, however, she painted. Between 1918 and 1934, largely working out of her "shanty," an outbuilding on the farm that she converted into a studio, O'Keeffe produced over two hundred paintings, in addition to numerous sketches and pastel works. She took the natural scenery around her as inspiration, capturing both grand views of the lake and surrounding mountains, and close-up studies of trees and flowers. In the fall, she would bring her canvases back from the Adirondacks to the city to finish and exhibit. Her nature-inspired abstractions were acclaimed, and O'Keeffe became a celebrity in the art world. The Lake George years are considered to be the most prolific period of her career.

This *seasonal* approach to work, in which you vary the intensity and focus of your efforts throughout the year, resonates with many who encounter it. O'Keeffe retreating to Lake George in the summer, where she would slowly unlock her creativity before returning to her busier city life in the fall, feels natural. As do the examples of seasonality we encountered in our earlier discussion of the great scientists: Isaac Newton pondering gravity in rural Lincolnshire, say, or Marie Curie recharging in the French countryside. The reality of our current moment is that professional seasonality of this type has become rare, especially in knowledge work. Outside of some full-time artists and writers, who like O'Keeffe can seek creativity in summer escapes, and educators, who work on an academic calendar, most people who toil at computer screens for a living do so twelve months out of the year with little variation in their intensity.

The fact that O'Keeffe's schedule feels exotic in our current moment, however, shouldn't obscure the reality that it's *our* unvarying approach to work that's the outlier here. As previously argued, for most of recorded human history, the working lives of the vast majority of people on earth were intertwined with agriculture, a (literally) seasonal activity. To work without change or rest all year would have seemed unusual to most of our ancestors. Seasonality was deeply integrated into the human experience.

This proposition argues that things don't have to be this way. Seasonality might be impossible in settings such as industrial manufacturing, but knowledge work is significantly more flexible. For those who work in cubicles instead of factories, there are more opportunities than you might at first imagine to vary your relationship with your work throughout the year. The key is to recognize that you don't need access to thirty-six acres of rural lakefront property to cultivate a beneficial seasonality. The concrete strategies that follow are designed to help those in standard contemporary jobs (e.g., not financially independent early twentieth-century artists) to reclaim at least some degree of natural variation in their efforts.

SCHEDULE SLOW SEASONS

In July 2022, when I was deep in the early stages of writing this book, a relevant trend went viral online. It started with a TikTok user named @ZKChillen posting a seventeen-second video in which soft piano music plays over scenes of New York City: a subway, a downtown street, a residential street, and then, for some reason, a child's bubble-blowing machine. "I recently heard about this idea of quiet quitting," the narrator begins, "where, you're not quitting your job, but quitting the idea of going above and beyond in your work." He goes on to reject the "hustle culture" belief that your work is your life. "The reality is that it's not," he concludes. "And your worth as a person is not defined by your labor."

As the original @ZKChillen video gained attention, more TikTok videos followed, most featuring young narrators making their own earnest declarations about their own embrace of quiet quitting. Predictably, the legacy press soon picked up on the trend. In early August, *The Guardian* published an article featuring a subhead that's notable for its casual nihilism: "The meaninglessness of modern work—and the pandemic—has led many to question their approach to their jobs." *The New York Times* and NPR followed with similar articles a couple of weeks later. Even *Shark Tank*'s Kevin O'Leary weighed in. (In case you're wondering, he thinks quiet quitting is a "really bad idea.")

As typically happens with internet trends, the quiet quitting movement eventually catalyzed a dogpile of one-upmanship and reactionary criticism. The "kids these days" crowd scoffed at the somber TikTok declarations. Your worth as a person might not be defined by your labor, they noted, but your salary as an employee certainly will be. Others found the idea to be unnecessarily passive-aggressive. If you're unhappy with your job, they argued, talk to your employer; to quiet quit just lets them off the hook for running a dysfunctional workplace. Soon the online activist types entered the fray to shame the original posters for not sufficiently acknowledging that some groups might struggle more than others to implement their advice. The old-school Far Left crowd, perhaps predictably, attempted to outflank the whole scrum by claiming that *any* discussion of this topic was itself a bourgeois exercise in futility, as the only real response to these issues is to dismantle capitalism.

If we're willing to push aside all of this digital posturing, at the core of quiet quitting is a pragmatic observation: you have more control than you think over the intensity of your workload. The tactics of quiet quitters are straightforward. They suggest, for example, that you don't volunteer for extra work, actually shut down at five o'clock, be comfortable saying no, and dilute an expectation of being constantly accessible over email and chat. As numerous quiet quitters report, these little changes can make a big difference on the psychological impact of your workload. This got me thinking. What if we stopped positioning quiet quitting as a general response to the "meaninglessness of work," and instead saw it as a more specific tactic to achieve seasonality? What if, for example, you decided to quiet quit a *single season* each year: maybe July and August, or that distracted period between Thanksgiving and the New Year? You wouldn't make a big deal about this decision. You would just, for lack of a better word, *quietly* implement it before returning without fanfare to a more normal pace.

For this idea to work, you should, if possible, arrange for major projects to wrap up before your simulated offseason begins, and wait to initiate major new projects until after it ends. An advanced tactic here is to take on a highly visible but low-impact project during this season that you can use to temporarily deflect new work that comes your way: "I'm happy to lead that internal review project, but I'm really focused this month on mastering this new marketing software, so let's wait until the New Year to get started." The key is to choose a deflection project that itself doesn't require a lot of collaboration, meetings, or urgent messages. Solo writing or research projects work well here.

If you work for yourself, of course, it's even easier to schedule slow seasons, as you don't have to worry about obfuscating your efforts. Indeed, as I'll argue later, the self-employed might consider going even further in their seasonality. For now, however, the key observation motivating this advice is that in most knowledge work employment situations, it's possible to surreptitiously slow down for a handful of months each year without any major consequences. A boss might notice if you're *always* deflecting projects, and a client might become concerned if you're *rarely* available to take on new work, but a month or two of a relatively slower pace is unlikely to be noticed. This strategy might not be as dramatic as Georgia O'Keeffe's languid summers at Lake George, but any sort of extended relief of this type, even if surreptitious, can make a major difference in the sustainability of your professional life.

DEFINE A SHORTER WORK YEAR

After the war, Ian Fleming, the novelist who would go on to write the James Bond spy thrillers, accepted a job with Kemsley Newspapers, a British media company best known for its ownership of the *Sunday Times*. Fleming was hired as its foreign manager, which put him in charge of the group's extensive network of overseas correspondents. He was well qualified for the job given his work with British Naval Intelligence—a position that had sent him around the world during the war. What's relevant to our purposes here, however, is less the details of Fleming's new employment than the contract he signed when he agreed to the position. Fleming made a deal with Kemsley that required him to work only ten months each year. The other two months would be taken as an annual vacation.

The motivation for this unusual agreement came in 1942, when Fleming, then a thirty-four-year-old commander, was sent to Jamaica as part of Operation Golden Eye, which was investigating potential German U-boat activity in the Caribbean. Fleming fell in love with the quiet and beauty of the island, and vowed that when the war was over, he'd find a way to return. His opportunity to make good on this promise came in 1946, when he learned of a fifteen-acre property, near the small port town of Oracabessa Bay, that had just gone up for sale. It wasn't stunning. A former donkey racetrack, the parcel was perched on a low headland, choked with tropical overbrush. But Fleming saw the potential. He telegraphed his agent to purchase the land, then cleared a plot to build a modest one-story house, with concrete floors and barely functioning plumbing. "The windows that look towards the sea are glassless," explained the travel writer Patrick Leigh Fermor, who visited Fleming's new home soon after its construction, "but equipped with outside shutters against the rain: enormous quadrilaterals . . . tame the elements, as it were, into an ever-changing fresco of which one can never tire." In honor of its inspiration, Fleming named his ramshackle estate Goldeneye.

This is why Fleming demanded two months' vacation in his contract. Each year, in fulfillment of his wartime promise to himself, he could now escape the dreary London winters to revel in the intentional slowness of life at Goldeneye. Initially, Fleming's retreats were purely hedonistic. When on the island, he would snorkel in the morning, in the inlet below his house, then turn his attention toward carousing—compensating, with a decidedly British upper-class vigor, for the darkness of his war experience. But then in 1952, at the urging of his new wife, Ann Charteris, Fleming took to writing while vacationing in Jamaica. She thought the activity would distract him from stress in his personal life.* That winter he wrote a draft of *Casino Royale*, the first James Bond novel. He went on to write a dozen more, always following the same general routine: outline the new novel's plot in London in the fall, write a full first draft at Goldeneye, working by the natural light of the Jamaican morning sun, and then, on returning home for the spring, complete the final editing before publication.

There's a romanticism to these stories about seasonal escapes that can be both immensely appealing and frustratingly impossible. Amid the tropical sun of the Caribbean winter, Fleming found inspiration to create one of the most enduring characters of mod-

---

* The specific stress was the fact that he had decided to marry his paramour after she became pregnant. It was the thought of marriage and fatherhood that sent Fleming into a funk, and led his new wife to recommend writing as a way to distract himself. Which is all to say, Ian Fleming is not someone you would want to study for lessons in character or morality.

ern genre literature, much as Georgia O'Keeffe discovered her signature artistic style in the southern Adirondacks. We can imagine a similar relief and creative charge if only we, too, could find a way to spend extended time away from our normal professional routines each year. But what was easy for someone like Fleming in postwar Britain seems impossibly distant from reality for most who toil in twenty-first-century knowledge work. Our only option seems to be the style of simulated seasonality described in the preceding strategy. This is better than nothing, of course, but not nearly as grandiose as escaping to the sea.

But is the Fleming model really so unobtainable today? Recall the example of Jenny Blake, whom I introduced in chapter 3. Like Fleming, Blake also takes off two months each year from her normal work. Unlike Fleming, however, she didn't have to leverage an elite social standing to curry favor with her employer. She runs her own modest corporate-training business, and simply set up her contracts to keep two months of her year clear. This reduces her income, of course, but as Blake explained to me when we discussed her setup, her goal is not to maximize money, but instead to maximize the quality of her life. Adjusting her budget to survive on roughly 20 percent less income each year was a profoundly fair trade for the benefits of an annual extended escape.

The writer Andrew Sullivan follows a similar model. Each August, he flees steamy Washington, DC, for a quaint Queen Anne–style cottage near the beach in Provincetown, at the northern tip of Cape Cod. The former editor of *The New Republic* now makes a living almost entirely off paid subscriptions to his Substack-based email newsletter. In theory, going quiet for weeks each summer is not optimal for someone who asks his audience to pay a monthly fee for his writing, but his subscribers don't seem to mind. Sullivan typically posts a midsummer essay about his impending vacation, often rich in enthusiastic anticipation. He then returns with new energy several weeks later, much to the satisfaction of both him and his readers.

Others who deploy a Fleming-style model are less regular about it than Blake or Sullivan. In my 2012 book, *So Good They Can't Ignore You*, for example, I profiled a freelance database developer named Lulu Young, whose breaks were more improvisational. In between major projects, she would often dedicate multiple weeks for travel or to pursue a new hobby. When I talked to her for my book, she had recently taken advantage of these gaps to master scuba diving, earn a pilot's license, and take a six-week trip to visit extended family in Thailand. Scattered among these bigger adventures, however, she also found joy in playing hooky for a day or two whenever the inspiration struck. "A lot of those days I would take a niece or nephew and have fun," she told me. "I went to the children's museum and zoo probably more than anyone else in the city."

For those who work standard office jobs, with bosses and normal hours, the dream of fully escaping for weeks or months at a time is difficult to achieve. If you work for yourself, however, the main force pushing you into year-round labor is likely cultural convention. Nothing terrible happened to Fleming, Blake, Sullivan, or Young when they decided to step back from their normal work for extended periods. They may have earned somewhat less money in the short term, but I'd wager that, to a person, they found this sacrifice to be very much worth it.

IMPLEMENT "SMALL SEASONALITY"

Seasonality doesn't refer only to slowing work for entire seasons. Varying your intensity at smaller timescales can also prove useful in achieving a more natural pace. The general goal for this proposition is to help you avoid working at a constant state of anxious high energy, with little change, throughout the entire year. Summering at Lake George can disrupt this unnatural rhythm, but so can taking off a random weekday once or twice a month. I call these latter, more modest efforts small seasonality. Here I'll detail four specific suggestions for implementing this philosophy. The hope is that once you've encountered a few of these examples, you'll more easily come up with numerous additional ideas on your own for injecting some much-needed variety into your pace.

No Meeting Mondays
Don't schedule appointments on Mondays. You don't need to make a public announcement about this decision. When people ask when you're free for a meeting or a call, just stop suggesting slots on that particular day. Because Monday represents only 20 percent of your available time, you can usually implement a meeting ban of this type without other people feeling like you're excessively unavailable. The benefit to you, however, is significant, because it allows a more gradual transition from the weekend back into the week. Sunday nights become less onerous when the cal-

endar for your next day is gloriously uncluttered. This reduced distraction also provides a consistent block of time each week to support progress on the types of hard but important projects that make your work more meaningful. Other days, of course, could also work just as well. Perhaps keeping Fridays clear of meetings works better for the pace of your particular job, or you find more value in maintaining a clear day in the middle of the week. The key to this idea is maintaining *some* bastion of peace amid an otherwise cluttered calendar.

See a Matinee Once a Month
There's something about entering a movie theater on a weekday afternoon that resets your mind. The context is so novel—"most people are at work right now!"—that it shakes you loose from your standard state of anxious reactivity. This mental transformation is cleansing and something you should seek on a regular basis. My suggestion is to try to put aside an afternoon to escape to the movies once per month, protecting the time on your calendar well in advance so it doesn't get snagged by a last-minute appointment. In most office jobs, no one is going to notice if once every thirty days or so you're gone for an afternoon. If someone asks where you were, just say you had a "personal appointment." Which is true. You should, of course, be reasonable in this planning to make sure that you're not missing something important. If an emergency comes up, or a week proves unusually filled with urgency, you can reschedule your mini-break for another day. If you feel guilty about this decision, it helps to remember all of the extra hours you've spent checking email in the evening or working on your

laptop over the weekend. Missing the occasional weekday afternoon only balances this ledger. To receive the benefits of this advice, it's not necessary that you see a film. Other activities can work as well. In my own experience, for example, I've also found similar benefits visiting museums and going on hikes. The key observation here is that even a modest schedule of weekday escapes can be sufficient to diminish the exhaustion of an otherwise metronome-regular routine.

Schedule Rest Projects

It can be stressful to start blocking out large chunks of time on your calendar for a major new project. Each new appointment you add represents less flexibility and more intense work in your near-future schedule. As your calendar continues to fill during busy periods, a sense of mild despair can arise. *How will I ever get this all done?* A clever way to balance this stress is to pair each major *work* project with a corresponding *rest* project. The idea is simple: after putting aside time on your calendar for a major work project, schedule in the days or weeks immediately following it time to pursue something leisurely and unrelated to your work. For example, perhaps you're a professor assigned to chair a faculty search committee during the upcoming spring. Perhaps this search will keep you busy until early May. To compensate, block off some afternoons later in that month to, say, finally watch Francis Ford Coppola's entire 1970s filmography, or learn a new language, or get your backyard workshop up and running once again. The key is to obtain a proportional balance. Hard leads to fun. The more hardness you face, the more fun you will enjoy soon after. Even if these rest projects are relatively small compared with the work that triggers them, this back-and-forth rhythm can still induce a sustaining experience of variation.

Work in Cycles

The software development company Basecamp is known for experimenting with innovative management practices. This is perhaps not surprising given that its cofounder and current CEO, Jason Fried, once published a book titled *It Doesn't Have to Be Crazy at Work*. One of Basecamp's more striking policies is the consolidation of work into "cycles." Each such cycle lasts from six to eight weeks. During those weeks, teams focus on clear and urgent goals. Crucially, each cycle is then followed by a two-week "cooldown" period in which employees can recharge while fixing small issues and deciding what to tackle next. "It's sometimes tempting to simply extend the cycles into the cooldown period to fit in more work," explains the Basecamp employee handbook. "But the goal is to resist this temptation."

This strategy embraces the natural seasonality of human effort. If Basecamp demanded that employees work with focus and urgency without break, their overall intensity would drop as exhaustion set in. When they instead regularly take time off between cycles, the work completed within the cycles achieves a higher level of quality. This latter scenario can end up producing better overall results than the former. It's also more sustainable for the employees involved.

Adopting some notion of cycles in your own work can be understood as a more structured implementation of both the rest project and seasonal quiet quitting strategies described above. You can propose the idea of making cycles a formal policy, pointing to the Basecamp handbook as support. Or, if you worry about how this suggestion will be received, you can quietly implement cycles without anyone knowing. The two-week cooldowns are too short for you to develop a reputation for shirking major initiatives. If anything, your increased intensity during the cycles themselves will probably be noticed more, shifting your employer's opinion of you toward the positive.

Interlude: Didn't Jack Kerouac Write *On the Road* in Three Weeks?

In 1959, Jack Kerouac appeared on *The Steve Allen Show*. The purpose of the segment was to promote an album the pair had just released, which featured Kerouac reading poetry over Allen's piano accompaniment. But the conversation started with a focus on the book, published two years earlier, that had made Kerouac famous: *On the Road*. Part impressionistic travelogue, part meditation on the philosophy of the Beat Generation, Kerouac's bestseller was defined by its jazz-inspired, fluid, stream-of-consciousness prose style. As its narrator, Sal Paradise, declares early in the book:

> The only people for me are the mad ones, the ones who are mad to live, mad to talk, mad to be saved, desirous of everything at the same time, the ones who never yawn or say a

commonplace thing, but burn, burn, burn like fabulous yellow roman candles.

The prose reads fast, like the thoughts were tumbling from Kerouac's brain onto a whirring typewriter's page. During his *Steve Allen* appearance, Kerouac buttresses this impression.

"Jack, got a couple of square questions, but I think the answer will be interesting," says Allen. "How long did it take you to write *On the Road*?"

"Three weeks," replies Kerouac.

"How many?"

"Three weeks."

As Kerouac goes on to elaborate, not only did he write his book in a three-week burst of frenzied energy, but he typed the manuscript onto a long continuous scroll of teletype paper, allowing him to compose his words without having to stop to swap fresh pages into his typewriter. As his brother-in-law, John Sampas, later detailed, "So he just rolled it along, almost breathlessly, quickly, fast, because the road is fast, to quote Jack."

I mention this well-worn tale of Jack Kerouac's inspired writing binge because it neatly captures an obvious objection to the second principle of slow productivity: sometimes a natural pace is too slow. Important work, this objection argues, requires sustained high-intensity, perhaps even obsessive, attention. To stretch out timelines and vary effort levels might be fine for making average efforts more tolerable, but it's not compatible with great work.

While it's undoubtedly true that important projects often require *temporary* periods of maximum intensity, I reject the idea that it's common for such projects to be fully completed in singular bursts of unwavering energy. Let's return, for example, to Kerouac. As his brother-in-law clarified in a 2007 NPR interview, when Kerouac told Allen he "wrote" *On the Road* in three weeks, what he really should have said is that he *typed* an initial draft of the manuscript in that amount of time. His full effort on the book stretched out over a much longer period: Kerouac worked on the novel in his journals between 1947 and 1949. Then, after his famous typing binge, he spent another six years completing six additional different drafts, trying to find a form that he could persuade a publisher to accept.

"Kerouac cultivated this myth that, you know, he was the spontaneous prose man and that everything that he ever put down was never changed," said Kerouac scholar Paul Marion. "[But] that's not true. I mean, he was really a supreme craftsman and devoted to writing and the writing process." Put another way, *On the Road* reads fast, but the pace at which it was composed, like most work that stands the test of time, was actually quite slow.

Proposition: Work Poetically

The poet Mary Oliver embodies the essence of working at a natural pace. Oliver, who had a troubled childhood, found escape in wandering the woods of her native Ohio. "I think it saved my life," she explained in a rare 2015 interview with Krista Tippett on

NPR. As Oliver elaborates, in search of light during this dark period, she took to noticing the poetic potential of the natural world during her extended rambles:

> Well, as I say, I don't like buildings. The only record I broke in school was truancy. I went to the woods a lot, with books—Whitman in the knapsack—but I also liked motion. So I just began with these little notebooks and scribbled things as they came to me, and then worked them into poems, later.

Oliver preserved this habit of outdoor walking and scribbling as she moved from Ohio to New England, where she settled and began publishing poems built on poignant but unembellished depictions of nature. Oliver's pace might have been unhurried, but her career cannot be described as anything short of immensely productive. Her fifth book of poetry, which came out in 1984, won a Pulitzer Prize. Her 1992 collection, *New and Selected Poems*, won the National Book Award. Oliver died in 2019 as one of the most widely read and beloved poets of the last century.

I mention Oliver to illustrate my final proposition about the second principle of slow productivity: sometimes cultivating a natural pace isn't just about the time you dedicate to a project, but also the context in which the work is completed. As the French philosopher Gaston Bachelard argues in *The Poetics of Space*, we shouldn't underestimate the ability of our surroundings to transform our cognitive reality. In discussing the role of a home, for example, Bachelard famously quipped, "Inhabited space transcends geometrical space." The stairway is not simply a collection of raised steps, arranged in a regular order, but instead where you played as a child with your siblings on rainy summer afternoons. Its surfaces and details are tangled into a complicated web of human experience.

These forces affect our professional efforts. Oliver's forest strolls weren't just about finding quiet. This outdoor context pulled on rich threads from her past, resulting in a perception of work that was more alive, varied, and natural in its pace than if she had spent those exact same hours writing at a perfectly nice home office desk. This proposition asks you to similarly assess the context of your most important work through this poetic lens. By taking care in your choice of physical spaces and rituals, you can not only transform the experience of your efforts into something more interesting and sustainable, but more fully tap into your latent brilliance. The trick, of course, is in identifying your own personalized version of Mary Oliver's long walks through the woods. The concrete advice that follows will help you in this pursuit.

MATCH YOUR SPACE TO YOUR WORK

An obvious heuristic for constructing a more effective space for your work is to match elements of your physical surroundings to what it is that you're trying to accomplish. Mary Oliver's nature-themed poetry, for example, was well served by long walks in the very style of woods that she described in her poems. Oliver is not alone in seeking this symmetry. Many writers leverage the details of their surroundings to support specific properties of their work. When composing *Hamilton*, for example, Lin-Manuel Miranda wrangled permission to write in the Morris-Jumel Mansion, the oldest surviving house in Manhattan, which served as both the headquarters for George Washington during the Battle of Harlem Heights and the home of Aaron Burr during his vice presidential years. "I love that we are just a bunch of layers above where all this shit went down," Miranda explained.

Meanwhile, in the forest behind his house in Woodstock, New York, Neil Gaiman built a spartan, eight-sided writing shed that sits on low stilts and offers views on all sides of endless trees. A picture of Gaiman's space, published online, reveals a simple desk, a notebook, and a pair of binoculars for observing wildlife. This setup makes sense for a writer who leverages close observation to inject an effective naturalism into his dark scenarios. Dan Brown, for his part, invested his *Da Vinci Code* fortune in a custom-built home near the seacoast in Rye Beach, New Hampshire, filled with the style of Gothic features one would expect to encounter in one of his popular thrillers. Push a button hidden in the library and a shelf swings open to reveal a display case. Touch the corner of a painting in the living room and a portal to a secret room appears. The inside of a bathroom door is decorated with a page from Leonardo da Vinci's notebook, written, as was Da Vinci's habit, in backward handwriting to conceal its content. When the door is closed, however, you can decipher the text by reading it through the bathroom mirror. You and I might find such a home unsettling and ostentatious. But if you make a living writing thrillers based on preposterous mysterious conspiracies, it might be exactly what you need to find your rhythm.

With some creativity, this same principle can be applied with similar effect to many nonwriting professions: an advertising executive might find inspiration in mid-century modern, *Mad Men*–style office decor; a music executive might fill her office with instruments; the engineer could emphasize half-assembled gadgets. Francis Ford Coppola has a long-standing habit of keeping soldering irons, switches, and diodes in his various production offices over the years. He used to love tinkering with electronic gizmos as a kid, and thinks the presence of the tools helps recenter him on the primal importance of building things from scratch. Whenever I see a generic home office, with its white bookcases and office-supply-store wall hangings, I can't help but think about all the ways in which its inhabitant could remake the setting into something more tailored to the work it supports.

STRANGE IS BETTER THAN STYLISH

In the late 1960s, the writer Peter Benchley and his wife, Wendy, were looking for a quiet place to live near New York City. They considered Princeton, New Jersey, but couldn't afford it, so they settled for Pennington, a small community eight miles to the west. It was here that Benchley got to work on his first novel, a sensationalist tale of a great white shark terrorizing a beach town. I've long been familiar with the connection between *Jaws* and Pennington because I grew up down the street from the house that the Benchleys had bought: a classic converted carriage home on a sizable property, framed by conifers. As a kid, doing homework in my attic bedroom, I sometimes liked to imagine that Benchley had looked out over a similar lawn down the street, crafting his iconic scenes.

It was only recently that I learned, to my dismay, that Benchley didn't actually write *Jaws* in his bucolic Pennington home. As John McPhee revealed in a 2021 *New Yorker* essay, he remembers Benchley during these years working in a rented space in the back of a furnace factory. A little digging, aided by the Hopewell Valley Historical Society, clarifies that it was Pennington Furnace Supply, Inc., situated on Brookside Avenue, off the north end of Pennington's Main Street. When later asked about it, Wendy Benchley still remembered the noise: "He had a desk right in the middle of this place where they were making furnaces," she said. "Bang! Bang! Bang!—and it didn't bother him."

Benchley isn't the only author to abandon a charming home to work in objectively worse conditions. Maya Angelou, for example, would rent hotel rooms to write, asking the staff to remove all artwork from the walls and to enter each day only to empty the wastebaskets. She'd arrive at six thirty in the morning, with a Bible, a yellow pad, and a bottle of sherry. No writing desk was necessary; she'd instead work lying across the bed, once explaining to George Plimpton, in an interview, how this habit led one of her elbows to become "absolutely encrusted" with calluses. David McCullough used to live in a beautiful white-shingled house in West Tisbury, on Martha's Vineyard. The residence included a nicely appointed home office, but McCullough preferred to write in a glorified garden shed in his backyard. John Steinbeck went one step further.

Late in his career, he spent his summers at a two-acre property in Sag Harbor. Steinbeck told his literary agent, Elizabeth Otis, that he would escape this waterfront paradise to instead write on his fishing boat, balancing a notebook on a portable desk.

I originally told these stories of eccentric writing spaces in an essay I published in the spring of 2021. At the time, the coronavirus pandemic was shifting beyond its acute emergency phase, and business communities were starting to wonder if remote work would become something more than just a short-term response to a health crisis. I meant my essay to serve as a warning relevant to this latter possibility. Professional writers, in some sense, were the original remote workers, and what you find when you study their habits, I noted, is that they often go way out of their way to find somewhere—*anywhere*—to work that's not inside their own homes. Even if it meant putting up with the clanging hammers of a furnace repair shop.

The problem is that the home is filled with the familiar, and the familiar snares our attention, destabilizing the subtle neuronal dance required to think clearly. When we pass the laundry basket outside our home office (aka our bedroom), our brain shifts toward a household-chores context, even when we would like to maintain focus on whatever pressing work needs to get done. This phenomenon is a consequence of the associative nature of our brains. Because the laundry basket is embedded in a thick, stress-inducing matrix of under-attended household tasks, it creates what the neuroscientist Daniel Levitin describes as "a traffic jam of neural nodes trying to get through to consciousness." In this context, work tumbles forward as one stress-inducing demand among many.

This is why Benchley retreated to the furnace factory and McCullough to his garden shed. They sought a more advantageous mental space to produce meaningful work. By calming their relational-memory system, they could slow their perception of time and allow their attention to mold itself more completely around a singular pursuit. What's important about these observations is that the aesthetics of their outside-the-home work spaces didn't really matter. Mary Oliver may have found depth in wandering the scenic New England woods, but Maya Angelou achieved a similar effect amid the forgettable blandness of cheap hotels. What counted was their disconnection from the familiar. A citadel to creative concentration need not be a literal palace. It just needs to be free of laundry baskets.

In my 2021 essay, I used these observations to argue for a separation between remote work and working from home. If organizations wanted to close down central offices, I proposed, they should reinvest this savings to help employees find places to work *near* their homes. By freeing these workers from the drag of the familiar, overall productivity and satisfaction would rise. Here I'm arguing that you keep something similar in mind during your individual efforts to create more poetic environments for your work. Strange is powerful, even if it's ugly. When seeking out where you work, be wary of the overly familiar.

RITUALS SHOULD BE STRIKING

The Mystery cults of ancient Greece are often misunderstood. As Karen Armstrong explains in her magisterial 2009 book, *The Case for God*, the Mystery rituals developed in the sixth century BCE were "neither a hazy abandonment of rationality nor a self-indulgent wallowing in mumbo jumbo." They were instead carefully constructed to induce specific psychological effects on the *mystai* (initiates) who performed them.

Consider, for example, the Eleusinian Mysteries, enacted annually in the town of Eleusis, just west of Athens, which celebrate the goddess Demeter's journey to Eleusis in search of her daughter Persephone. Armstrong notes that Eleusis had likely been the site of some sort of autumn festival since the Neolithic era, but it was in the sixth century that the town built a massive new cult hall to house a more formalized and powerful experience. Each fall a new group of mystai would volunteer to participate in the ritual. They began in Athens with two days of fasting. They then sacrificed a piglet in honor of Persephone and began the roughly twenty-mile walk to Eleusis. The initiates from the previous year's ritual would join the new mystai on the journey, harassing and threatening them while repetitively calling out to Dionysus, god of wine and ecstasy, with the goal, as Armstrong writes, of eventually "driving the crowd into a frenzy of excitement." After finally arriving in Eleusis after nightfall, the mystai, exhausted and anxious, were led through the streets by torchlight, increasing their sense of disorientation before they were finally herded into the complete darkness of the initiation hall.

The details of the ceremony that unfolded inside the hall were held in secrecy, so we have only scraps and suggestions of its details. There were likely animal sacrifices and mystical revelations. Armstrong argues there was also probably a "shocking event," like a child being prepared to be pushed into a fire, only to be saved at the last moment—all of this taking place against a backdrop of alternating darkness and light, flickering flames, and unnatural sounds. By some reports, the events culminated "joyfully" with a living tableau depicting Persephone's return from the underworld and reunion with her mother.

As Armstrong explains, the Eleusinian Mysteries were not about conveying a rational doctrine that initiates were asked to believe. If you wrote out a description of the full ceremony, it would seem, from an objective perspective, to be silly and random. The Mysteries were instead about the psychological state they induced. Many participants reported coming out of the rituals no longer afraid of death. Some described the experience as a moment of divine possession. "In a superb summary of the religious process, Aristotle would later make it clear that the *mystai* did not go to Eleusis to learn (*mathein*) anything," summarizes Armstrong, "but to have an experience (*pathein*) and a radical change of mind (*diatethenai*)."

In this account of ancient Greek Mystery cults, we learn something important about rituals in general. Their power is found not in the specifics of their activities but in the transformative effect these activities have on the mind. The more striking and notable the behaviors, the better chance they have of inducing useful changes. Mary Oliver's long walks through the woods provide a good case study. As her mileage increased and she journeyed deeper into a forest setting that pulled on so many emotional anchor points, her mental state transformed into something rawer and more receptive. Presumably, if she had instead simply sat just inside the wood's edge, the impact would have been blunted. The ritual of the long walk was as necessary as its setting to spark her creativity.

The options for these poetic ceremonies are vast. In *Daily Rituals*, Mason Currey catalogs a variety of eccentric, mind-transforming routines developed by dozens of great thinkers and creators. David Lynch would order a large chocolate milkshake at a Bob's Big Boy restaurant. He would then leverage the resulting sugar rush to extract idea after idea from his subconscious, often scrawling them onto napkins. N. C. Wyeth would wake at 5:00 a.m. to chop wood for over an hour before hiking up to his studio on a hill. Anne Rice wrote *Interview with the Vampire* largely at night, catching up on her sleep during the day—the quiet darkness putting her into the right mindset to craft her gothic tale. When living near the French country village of Ain, Gertrude Stein would wake at 10:00 a.m., drink a cup of coffee, and then take a bath in an oversize tub. After getting dressed, she would drive through the surrounding countryside with her partner, Alice B. Toklas, looking for an auspicious place to work. Once such a site was found, Stein would settle onto a camp stool with a pencil and pad of paper and begin to write.

My advice here has two parts. First, form your own personalized rituals around the work you find most important. Second, in doing so, ensure your rituals are sufficiently striking to effectively shift your mental state into something more supportive of your goals. The second principle of productivity asks that you work at a more natural pace. It's suitable that this suggestion about rituals closes this chapter, as there are few strategies that will more effectively transform your perception of time, pushing your experience away from anxiety and toward the more sublimely natural, than to add a dash of poetic mystery to your efforts.

5 OBSESS OVER QUALITY

The Third Principle of Slow Productivity

In the early 1990s, an unusual scene began unfolding on a side street near Pacific Beach, a San Diego surf spot popular with longboarders. On Thursday nights, a crowd would gather at the Inner Change Coffeehouse. At first the group was small. As the weeks passed, it grew until it took up all of the café's modest capacity. The overflow crowd piled onto the sidewalk outside the venue, looking through a storefront plate-glass window and listening to a small set of speakers set up to relay the music from inside.

The draw was a nineteen-year-old singer-songwriter who went by her first name alone: Jewel. At the time, Jewel was living out of her car, barely getting by with odd jobs and busking on the San Diego beachfront. Her existence was precarious. Not long before her remarkable run at the Inner Change Coffeehouse, for example, she had found herself sick with a kidney infection, feverish and vomiting in the back seat of her car outside a hospital emergency room that had turned her away due to lack of insurance. A doctor who had watched the scene unfold found her in the parking lot and gave her a free course of antibiotics—likely saving her life.

What rescued Jewel during this period was her ability to perform epic folk-style music sets alone onstage with her guitar. This was a skill she'd been cultivating most of her life. When Jewel was young, her parents had a musical act that they would perform at various tourist hotels in Anchorage, Alaska. Jewel started joining her parents onstage at the age of five, wearing a handmade Swiss outfit, to yodel. (Her paternal grandparents had emigrated to Alaska from Switzerland.) She practiced relentlessly to master the technique, providing her a foundation of vocal control that she would later use to great effect in her professional career.

Jewel's parents divorced when she was eight. Her mom left, leaving her dad to raise the kids on his own. He retreated to the family homestead, located outside the halibut fishing hub of Homer, Alaska. Soon the family was surviving off their earnings from music alone, with Jewel taking her mom's part in the act, singing harmony to her dad's lead, while her brother worked the soundboard. The performances in fancy hotels were gone, with the family now instead playing long sets at "honky-tonks, juke joints, restaurants, lumberjack haunts, and veterans' bars." Jewel remembers liking the biker bars the best, as the grizzled men and their hardened wives were protective of her.

The rest of Jewel's childhood unfolded haphazardly. She bounced back and forth between Homer and Anchorage, continuing to tour with her dad all over the state. They visited cities as well as outposts in the interior, once putting on a memorable stretch of performances for isolated Inuit villages. As a teenager, now living on her own in a small cabin, and, believe it or not, commuting to her job in town on horseback (she didn't yet have a driver's license), Jewel met a dance instructor named Joe who was putting on a two-week clinic in Homer. Joe turned out to also be a teacher at the prestigious Interlochen Arts Academy, located on 1,200 manicured acres just outside Traverse City, Michigan. Impressed by Jewel's voice, developed into an early maturity through a childhood of marathon performances, Joe helped her navigate Interlochen's application and audition process. Jewel was accepted, but it took her some time to adjust to the new culture: soon after arriving, she was called to the dean's office, where she was informed that it wasn't appropriate to walk around campus with a skinning knife strapped to her leg.

Jewel received professional voice training at Interlochen, and was, more generally, exposed for the first time to art as a serious endeavor. Perhaps equally important, it was during this period that she began songwriting. Unable to afford travel back to Alaska during school holidays, she took to hitchhiking with her guitar during the days when the classrooms were closed. It was on these trips that she wrote the early versions of songs like "Who Will Save Your Soul" and "You Were Meant for Me," using the sights and sounds of her travels for inspiration.

After graduating, Jewel once again wandered, eventually making her way to San Diego, where her mother had settled. They lived together for a while in a house that they couldn't afford and that they eventually lost. This is when Jewel moved into her car, finding a spot to park near a nice-looking flowering tree, not far from Pacific Beach. It was while walking back to this parking spot one afternoon that she first stumbled across the Inner Change Coffeehouse, which looked like it had seen better days. Jewel introduced herself to the owner, Nancy. They struck up a conversation, and Nancy revealed that she was planning to shutter her struggling business. On a whim, Jewel made her an offer:

"Do you think you can stay open for two more months?" Jewel asked.

"Why?" Nancy replied.

"If I bring people in, can I keep the door money, you can keep all the coffee and food, and, like, we'll try to make it together."

Nancy agreed to the plan, and Jewel took her guitar to the San Diego waterfront to promote the show. When people would stop to listen to her singing, she would tell them to come see her at Inner Change that Thursday night. For her first performance at the coffeehouse, Jewel managed to persuade only a handful of surfers to attend. The minuscule size of the crowd didn't stop Jewel from "bleeding my heart out." As she recalls:

> When these people came, I just bore my soul. I just didn't pull a punch. And they liked me. I know that sounds superficial, but it wasn't. It was so authentically me. . . . It was so raw. And people would cry. And I would cry. And it was such a real connection. For the first time in my life, I had a real meaningful human connection and it wasn't scary, it felt good.

Jewel's life up to this point had been carved by the tangled forces of talent and pain. When she decided to bare her soul, the results were authentic, raw, and by most accounts, spectacular. Word spread quickly. The first performance might have been to an audience of only two or three surfers, but the audiences began doubling week after week. It took only six months before fans were crowding the sidewalk outside the café. Soon after that, record executives began showing up in limousines to hear the young sensation. "Every label came down, every label," Jewel recalled. Then they began flying her to meetings in fancy offices. A bidding war erupted, eventually leading to a *million-dollar* signing bonus being put on the table.

It's here that Jewel made the move that will render her story relevant to our discussion of slow productivity. Overwhelmed by this tumultuous turn in her life—feeling simultaneously ambitious and terrified—she came to an unexpected decision. She would sign a deal, but she didn't want the money. "I turned down the advance," she recalled. "I turned down a million-dollar bonus. As a homeless kid."

When Jewel first began attracting attention at the Inner Change Coffeehouse, she didn't have a manager or a lawyer. Intimidated by the executives taking her out for dinner after her Thursday night shows, she went to the library and found a book titled *All You Need to Know About the Music Business*. It was here that she learned that signing bonuses were really just loans that you have to pay back through your earnings. Jewel did some quick math and realized that in order for the record label to recoup a million-dollar bonus, she would have to sell a huge number of records almost immediately. This seemed unlikely given the fact that she was a folk act during a period when grunge dominated the industry, and that she was less than a year into her career as a professional performer, much of which had been spent playing at the same coffeehouse.

"I had to put myself in an environment and a position to win as a singer-songwriter," she recalled thinking, and the way to do that was to be cheap. If she didn't cost the label much money, Jewel reasoned, they would be less likely to drop her if she wasn't an immediate hit. This in turn would provide her the freedom needed to sharpen her craft and pursue something new and exceptional with her music. "I was just doing it to put myself in a position to make my art first," she later explained. "To not leverage my art unduly." She adopted a motto for her intentional approach: "Hardwood grows slowly."

This focus on quality over quick returns became obvious with her choice of producer. Her label, Atlantic Records, presented twenty different names for Jewel to consider, many of them hotshots in the industry, valued for their ability to spin pop gold. Jewel, however, was going for something different: a more raw and authentic sound, so she turned down all twenty choices. Around this period, Jewel and her manager were listening to Neil Young's *Harvest Moon*. She realized that *this* was the sound she wanted. They turned the CD over to discover the name of the producer: Ben Keith. Jewel had her manager call Keith and ask if he would work on the album. He agreed. Jewel left the bustle of LA to spend several weeks at Neil Young's ranch in Northern California, working on tracks for her record with Young's all-star backing band, the Stray Gators.

When Jewel's first album, *Pieces of You*, was finally released in 1995, it fell flat. "Radio hated me, they hated me, vehemently hated me," Jewel explained. "I mean, imagine Nirvana and Soundgarden, and then you hear a song like 'You Were Meant for Me,' and you go, 'No.'" But because she didn't cost the record label much money to support, they didn't drop her. This allowed Jewel to focus her energy on building a fan base through touring, which she began to do at a relentless clip, taking on what she described as "a tremendous workload." True to her plan, Jewel kept her expenses low. Instead of having a tour bus and tour manager, she traveled cheap in a rental car and performed without a band. At one point, she even signed on with a group called Earth Jam, which would provide her free transportation to her evening gigs if she agreed to participate in an environmentally themed showcase they put on for local high schools during the day.

As sales continued to stay flat, pressure mounted for Jewel to pivot toward a more lucrative style. At one point, she retreated to a recording studio in Woodstock, New York, to start recording a second album that featured edgier, more angsty lyrics that better fit the grunge-inspired alternative music of the era. She also agreed to her label's plan to have a hotshot producer named Juan Patiño, famous at the time for his work on Lisa Loeb's hit single, "Stay," recut "You Were Meant for Me" into a faster paced, more poppy style. ("I hated it" was Jewel's secret reaction to the Patiño cut.) Fortunately, it was exactly at the moment she was suffering these temptations that Neil Young called and asked Jewel to open for him and Crazy Horse during their current tour. Standing offstage, waiting for a show to begin, Young noticed Jewel's anxiety. He asked her what was wrong. She opened up about all the pressures and stress she was feeling. He gave her a critical piece of advice in response: "Do not ever write for radio. Ever."

Jewel listened to Young and returned to her plan of taking it slow and focusing on quality. She discarded the partially complete second album and shelved the Patiño version of "You Were Meant for Me." She instead redoubled her touring efforts, focusing on college campuses and college radio stations. This strategy finally began to bear fruit, and her first single, "Who Will Save Your Soul," found a fleeting position on the charts. She then translated all that she had learned from her intensive touring to cut a new and improved version of "You Were Meant for Me." She felt that she was too nervous on the original track, recorded early in her professional career at Neil Young's ranch, and that her discomfort playing with a band came through. Her new version was looser and more soulful, featuring her longtime friend Flea, from the Red Hot Chili Peppers, playing bass. Jewel's album sales twitched. Then trended upward. After she released a sultry video for "You Were Meant for Me," they exploded. The album went from selling a few thousand copies over its first year to close to a million copies each month. "It was staggering," Jewel recalled. "A tiny snowball in hell had caught enough momentum to create a tide change." Hardwood grows slowly.

Jewel's strategy of prioritizing art over fame provides a nice case study of the third and final principle of slow productivity: obsess over quality. As captured in the definition below, when you concentrate your attention on producing your best possible work, a more humane slowness becomes inevitable:

> ### PRINCIPLE #3: OBSESS OVER QUALITY
>
> *Obsess over the quality of what you produce, even if this means missing opportunities in the short term. Leverage the value of these results to gain more and more freedom in your efforts over the long term.*

The sections that follow next in this chapter will unpack the fruitful connection between quality and slow productivity highlighted by Jewel's story. Quality demands that you slow down. Once achieved, it also helps you take control of your professional efforts, providing you the leverage needed to steer even further away from busyness. These explanatory sections will then be followed by a pair of propositions that offer pragmatic advice for introducing an obsession with quality into your own life.

There's a reason why this principle is presented last: it's the glue that holds the practice of slow productivity together. Doing fewer things and working at a natural pace are both absolutely necessary components of this philosophy, but if those earlier principles are implemented on their own, without an accompanying obsession with quality, they might serve only to fray your relationship to work over time—casting your professional efforts as an imposition that you must tame. It's in the obsession over what you're producing that slowness can transcend its role as just one more strategy on the arid battlegrounds of work-life wars and become a necessary imperative—an engine that drives a meaningful professional life.

From Record Deals to Email Freedom; or, Why Knowledge Workers Should Obsess Over Quality

The importance of quality is crystal clear in the context of artists. Jewel was really good at singing, so Atlantic Records offered her a million-dollar bonus. When we shift our attention to knowledge work, these connections become obfuscated. Most of us don't do just one thing, such as singing or acting in movies, on which our professional performance is assessed. The sine qua non of knowledge work is instead the juggling of many different objectives. As a professor, I teach classes, I submit grants, I deal with the paperwork involving existing grants, I supervise students, I sit on committees, I write papers, I travel to present these papers and struggle to format them for publication. In the moment, everything seems important. Most other jobs in this sector are similarly varied.

Even in knowledge work, however, if we look closer, we can often find hidden among our busy to-do lists one or two core activities that really matter most. When professors go up for promotion, for example, most of what occupies our days falls away from consideration. The decision comes down to exhaustive confidential letters, solicited from prominent scholars, that discuss and debate the importance and impact of our research on our field. In the end, great research papers are what matter for us. If we haven't notably advanced our academic specialty, no amount of to-do list martyrdom can save us. Other knowledge work positions have similar core activities lurking inside the whirlwind. Just as Jewel had to be a great singer, the graphic designer ultimately has to produce effective artwork, the development director has to bring in dollars, the marketer has to sell products, and the manager has to lead a well-functioning team.

The third and final principle of slow productivity asks that you obsess over the quality of the core activities in your professional life. The goal here is not about becoming really good for the sake of being really good at your job (though this is nice). As I'll argue next, you should be focused on the quality of what you produce because quality turns out to be connected in unexpected ways to our desire to escape pseudo-productivity and embrace something slower.

The flashiest part of Jewel's story is the million-dollar signing bonus that she was offered. What's more important for our purposes, however, is the fact that she turned it down. As explained, she realized that she needed to push her art to a higher level of quality to support a long career in the music industry. Turning down the money made her cheap to the record label and therefore bought her time to improve. This same effect applies to many different fields: obsessing over quality often demands that you slow down, as the focus required to get better is simply not compatible with busyness.

In the context of knowledge work, perhaps the most famous example of quality demanding slowness is Steve Jobs's triumphant return to Apple. When Jobs started as interim CEO in 1997, the company had just come off a quarter in which its sales fell 30 percent. Jobs quickly assessed that Apple's problem was connected to its sprawling product lines. (In response to retailer demands, the company had developed numerous different variations of its core computers, including a dozen different versions of its once-vaunted Macintosh.) According to Jobs's biographer, Walter Isaacson, Jobs began asking top managers a simple question: "Which ones do I tell my friends to buy?" When they couldn't provide a clear answer, he made the decision to simplify their product line down to only four computers: a desktop and laptop for business users and a desktop and laptop for casual users. There would be no confusion about which Apple machine was right for you.

Equally important, this simplification allowed Apple to focus its efforts on quality and innovation: making its small number of products stand out. This was the period, for example, in which Apple's colorful, bulbous iMac and whimsical clamshell iBook were released. The decision to trade complexity for quality worked. During Jobs's first fiscal year, when his plan was still being implemented, Apple lost over a billion dollars. The next year, it turned a profit of $309 million. "Deciding what not to do is as important as deciding what to do," Jobs explained.

This relationship between quality and slowness exists at smaller scales as well. My reader survey included numerous case studies of individuals who discovered that the pursuit of quality demanded simplicity. A consultant named Chris, for example, pushed the quality of his team's client work "much higher" by relegating email to one hour in the morning and a half hour in the evening, while also demanding that his team observe a three-hour deep-work period each afternoon with no meetings, messages, or calls allowed. A research director named Abby told me a similar story. She had been "fractured across a million projects," which she found exhausting, so when she moved to a new position, she decided to adopt a different strategy: she would focus her energy on exactly two major goals. This clarity allowed her to step away from a more frenetic, overloaded busyness. "Keeping those two big-picture goals in mind helps me figure out what to say no to and how to pace myself," she explained. A nonprofit consultant named Bernie also leveraged a "clearly defined purpose/vision" to slow down and focus his work. As he summarized, "A little quality work every day will produce more and more satisfying results than frantic work piled on top of frantic work."

The first principle of slow productivity argues that you should do fewer things because overload is neither a humane nor pragmatic approach to organizing your work. This third principle's focus on quality, however, transforms professional simplicity from an option to an imperative. Once you commit to doing something very well, busyness becomes intolerable. In other words, this third principle helps you stick with the first. As we'll see next, however, as we return to the story of Jewel, this relationship between quality and doing less also includes another, more subtle layer.

In 1998, after the meteoric success of her debut album, Jewel released her follow-up effort, *Spirit*, which debuted at number three on the Billboard charts and sold over 350,000 copies in its first week. To support the record, Jewel embarked on a six-month international tour. Around this same time, she made her film debut in Ang Lee's *Ride with the Devil*. Pressure mounted for her to move permanently to Los Angeles, where she could audition for more movie roles between major album releases. It was at this moment of peak momentum, however, that Jewel began to have second thoughts. "I just wasn't sure I liked what my career had become," she writes in her memoir. "It had gotten bigger and bigger until it was a machine that consumed me." Breaking away from the strike-while-the-iron-is-hot logic of the entertainment industry, Jewel decided to slow down. Instead of moving to LA, she relocated to a ranch in Texas with her boyfriend at the time, the rodeo rider Ty Murray, explaining, "I didn't need to be any more rich or famous." She never again went on an overseas tour.

As we previously established, pursuing higher quality requires you to slow down. In this story of Jewel stepping off the industry fast track, we flip the arrow of influence between these two concepts. To better explain what I mean here, let's leave the rarefied world of international concert tours and turn our attention instead to a modest modern-style home, hidden away at the end of a long drive, within the temperate rainforest of Vancouver Island. It's here that we find Paul Jarvis. It's hard to describe exactly what it is that Jarvis does for a living, other than it seems to involve a computer screen and that it allows him to spend notable amounts of time outside, going on hikes and fiddling with his gardens. In some sense, as we'll see, this inscrutability is the point.

I first encountered Jarvis when his editor sent me a copy of his 2019 book, *Company of One*. I was taken by the boldness of its premise: don't scale your business. If you're fortunate enough for your entrepreneurial endeavors to begin to succeed, he argues, leverage this success to gain more freedom instead of more revenue. This dynamic is captured well by a simplified thought experiment. Imagine that you charge $50 an hour as a web designer. Assuming forty hours of work a week, fifty weeks a year, this works out to a $100,000 annual salary. Now imagine that after a few years at this level, your skills expand and the demand for your services increases. The standard move would be to scale your business. If you hired multiple designers, you could grow it to the point where it was bringing in millions in annual revenue and yielding you a salary that was well above $100,000 a year. If you continued this growth, you might even end up one day with an enterprise valuable enough to sell for a healthy seven-figure payday.

In his book, Jarvis asks that you consider an alternative. What if after your reputation spread, instead of growing the business, you increased your hourly rate to $100? You could now maintain your same $100,000 a year salary while working only twenty-five weeks a year—creating a working life with a head-turning amount of freedom. It would of course be nice to earn a seven-figure payday ten years from now, but given all the stress and hustle required to build a business of the necessary size, it's not clear that you would really end up in a more remarkable place than the scenario in which you're right away able to reduce your work by half.

Jarvis's philosophy is reflected in the decisions he made in his own professional life. He studied computer science in college but also had a natural feel for visual design. During the first internet boom of the 1990s, these two skills proved to be the perfect combination for success in the emerging medium of website design. Jarvis produced several eye-catching sites on his own, which soon led to job offers. Before long, he was a busy web designer living in downtown Vancouver "in a glass cube in the sky." He felt the normal pressure to grow his small business: more revenue would mean a better apartment and more prestige. But even though his growing skills would support this well-trod professional path, his heart wasn't in it. "My wife and I had just had enough of the city," he recalled in a 2016 interview. "We did our time in the rat race, and we wanted something different." Recognizing that his freelance design work could be accomplished from any location with an internet connection, they moved to the woods outside Tofino, on the Pacific shore of Vancouver Island, so his wife, who was a surfer, could enjoy the sleepy town's famed breaks.

As they discovered, frugality is easy when you're living in the woods of Vancouver Island, as there aren't that many opportunities to spend money. "When you're remote, there's nobody to do things for you, so you have to do a lot for yourself," Jarvis explained. Freed from the need to increase his income to keep up with city expenses, Jarvis leveraged his growing skills to keep his work responsibilities flexible and contained. At first, he focused on freelance design contracts. Because he was in demand, he could keep his hourly rate high and his number of projects small. Eventually, tired of deadlines and client communication, he explored ways to further transform his notable skills and reputation to achieve even more slowness. He began experimenting with online courses aimed at various niche topics relevant to the freelancer community. He also began hosting a pair of podcasts and turned his attention to quietly launching software tools aimed at narrow markets, including, most recently, Fathom Analytics, an alternative to Google Analytics that better preserves user privacy.

It's hard to detail the full list of things Jarvis has worked on in recent years, as his various ideas seem to come and go, leaving behind a trail of broken URLs and out-of-date websites: which is, of course, exactly what you'd expect from someone who isn't trying to build the next Microsoft but is instead pursuing *just enough* work to engage his curiosity while supporting his slow, inexpensive lifestyle. "I typically rise with the sun and haven't ever owned an alarm clock," Jarvis explains. "While my coffee brews, I stand at a window and watch wild rabbits frolic, hummingbirds buzz, or the occasional crafty raccoon attempt to ruin my garden."

Both Jewel and Paul Jarvis discovered a similar lesson in their careers. The marketplace doesn't care about your personal interest in slowing down. If you want more control over your schedule, you need something to offer in return. More often than not, your best source of leverage will be your own abilities. What makes Jarvis's story so heartening is its demonstration that these benefits of "obsessing" over quality don't necessarily require that you dedicate your entire life to the blinkered pursuit of superstardom. Jarvis didn't sell fifteen million records; he instead became, over time, good at core skills that were both rare and valuable in the particular field in which he worked. But this was enough, when leveraged properly, to enable significantly more simplicity in his professional life. We've become so used to the idea that the only reward for getting better is moving toward higher income and increased responsibilities that we forget that the fruits of pursuing quality can also be harvested in the form of a more sustainable lifestyle.

We've now detailed two complementary ways that an obsession with quality supports the rejection of pseudo-productivity: it both *demands* and *enables* slowness. Motivated by these realities, the propositions that follow will help you rebuild your working life around doing the core things better. They'll also guide you toward better leveraging the opportunities this will provide to simplify. As you consider this more concrete advice, keep in mind the example of Chris the consultant stripping meetings and email out of the heart of the workday, or Paul Jarvis walking the tree-lined path to his extensive gardens at his house in Tofino. Obsessing over quality isn't just about being better at your job. It's instead a secret weapon of sorts for those interested in a slower approach to productivity.

Proposition: Improve Your Taste

One of the more pragmatic statements ever made about producing quality work came from Ira Glass, the creator and host of the influential NPR show *This American Life*. In an interview about radio production and storytelling that has since been extensively shared online, Glass offers the following advice:

> All of us who do creative work, we get into it because we have good taste. . . . But it's like there's a gap. That for the first couple years that you're making stuff, what you're making, isn't so good . . . it's not quite that good. . . . If you're just starting off and you're entering into that phase, you gotta know it's totally normal and the most important possible thing you can do is do a lot of work. . . . Put yourself on a deadline so that every week or every month you know you're gonna finish one story. . . . It's only by actually going through a volume of work that you're actually going to catch up and close that gap, and the work you're making will be as good as your ambitions.

Glass correctly identifies "taste" as critical for achieving quality. The act of creation can be decomposed into a series of spontaneous eruptions of new possibilities, which must then be filtered against some ineffable understanding of what works and what doesn't—the visceral intuition that we call taste. In *Bird by Bird*, the novelist Anne Lamott elegantly captures this rhythm of creation. "You find yourself back at the desk, staring blankly at the pages you filled yesterday. And there on page four is a paragraph with all sorts of life in it, smells and sounds and voices and colors," she writes. "You don't care about those first three pages; those you will throw out, those you needed to write to get to that fourth page, to get to that one long paragraph that was what you had in mind when you started, only you didn't know that." Taste, in this process, acts as the compass that guides you toward the peaks and away from the valleys in the fitness landscape of possible creations.

In his exposition, Glass focuses on the gap that often exists between taste and ability—especially early on in a creative career. It's easier to learn to recognize what's good, he notes, than to master the skills required to meet this standard. I can see brilliance in the epic three-minute tracking shot that opens Paul Thomas Anderson's *Boogie Nights*, but I would have no idea how to film something that good on my own. There's a fundamental frustration embedded in this reality. Your taste can guide you toward the best work you're capable of producing at the moment, but it can also fuel a sense of disappointment in your final result. Glass argues that it's in our desire to squelch this uneasy self-appraisal—to diminish the distance between our taste and our ability—that improvement happens. His exhortation to those just beginning their careers is to keep putting in the work, as it's only through this deliberate effort that the gap will close.

All of this is solid advice, but it misses an equally critical element: the development of your taste in the first place. "All of us who do creative work, we get into it because we have good taste," he says. But where does this discernment come from? In other interviews, Glass sometimes discusses his frustrations with the low quality of his early radio segments. In a 2022 conversation on Michael Lewis's podcast, for example, Glass dissects a radio report he recorded in 1986 on the seventy-fifth anniversary of the Oreo cookie. He tells Lewis that the segment is "utterly mediocre" and "not a great story." This might at first seem a good illustration of the gap between taste and ability that Glass argues all creatives must overcome. But as his conversation with Lewis continues, it becomes clear that Glass didn't necessarily realize the inadequacy of the piece at the time when he recorded it. "I remember when I finished it, I was like, I remember feeling like, okay, I've finally got it, I finally know what I'm doing," he recalls.

What we encounter here is a more nuanced story about producing quality work. Glass's taste in 2022 is more refined than it was in 1986. His success came not only from a drive to meet his own high standards, but also from his efforts to *improve* those standards over time. When we return to the example of novelists, we find this reality reflected in the ubiquity of MFA programs in the backgrounds of acclaimed new writers. I researched, for example, the biographies of the five finalists for the most recent PEN/Hemingway Award for Debut Novel (at the time of my writing this chapter), a prestigious honor in literary fiction. Of these five finalists, four of them attended or taught in MFA programs before publishing their award-caliber books. The power of MFA programs is not in their explicit writing instruction, which is minimal, but instead in the elite community they provide to the developing novelist. When you spend two years reading and critiquing and admiring work by other young writers pushing their prose in new and interesting directions, your standards for what writing can achieve sharpen. You don't have to attend one of these programs, of course, to succeed in literature. Colson Whitehead, for example, is undoubtedly one of the most talented novelists of his generation, and yet he never studied beyond his bachelor's degree. But there's a reason why MFA programs are so common among successful writers: they provide an effective training regimen for literary taste.

When we idolize an Ira Glass–style obsession with quality, we often overlook the importance of developing our internal filters first. It's more exciting to focus on effort, drive, and diligence—but no amount of grinding away at your proverbial radio program or novel manuscript will lead to brilliance if you don't yet have a good understanding of what brilliance could mean. This proposition seeks to correct this omission. What follows is a collection of practical suggestions designed to help improve your understanding of what's possible in your field.

BECOME A CINEPHILE

One of the best things I've done recently to improve my writing quality is to watch the Quentin Tarantino movie *Reservoir Dogs*. To understand this claim, it's important to first understand that I've always been a fan of movies. Before we had kids, my wife and I used to see almost every major film release. In that pre-Netflix era, we also saw many of the more interesting documentary features that made their way through Boston's independent theater scene. It wasn't until I turned forty, however, that I thought it might be fun to study the art of filmmaking more systematically. In my book *Digital Minimalism*, I had written extensively about the importance of high-quality leisure activities. It wasn't until I hit that notable midlife birthday that I realized I wasn't following my own advice. Between my work as a professor and writer, my role as a father, and a tendency to fill any remaining free time with reading, I didn't really have anything I could identify as a serious hobby, so I thought, given my preexisting interest, I would give cinema a try.

I began by reading an introductory textbook on film theory but found it wasn't very helpful. It talked about concepts like editing and sound in abstract, simplified terms, serving as a glossary of sorts for more advanced courses that would follow in a typical degree program. Next, I tried Roger Ebert's book *The Great Movies*, which contained one hundred essays about one hundred movies that the late Pulitzer Prize–winning critic thought were seminal. This was more effective, as it got straight to specific praise about specific movies. Tarantino's essay collection, *Cinema Speculation*, also proved an important source of insight into what makes a good movie good and, equally important, what makes a fun movie fun.

The most useful exercise of all, however, was to simply pick a well-regarded movie, read a half dozen or so reviews and essays on it, and then watch the full film. An advanced twist I discovered was to look for articles on the movie in question in cinematography magazines or forums, as these often included gratifyingly detailed discussions of lens and framing techniques. Did you know, for example, that in *Mad Max: Fury Road*, director George Miller and cinematographer John Seale (who came out of retirement for the film) purposefully positioned the focal point of every shot in the center of the frame, defying cinematic convention but making the fast-cut action much more legible to the audience? Learning about this center-framing technique, in an article written by cinematographer Vashi Nedomansky, completely changed my appreciation for Miller's masterpiece.

This brings us back to *Reservoir Dogs*. My project of self-education drew me inevitably to Tarantino's classic 1992 film, which revived the independent film scene after a decade of stultifying, safe Hollywood blockbusters. As I read about his use of nonlinear narratives and reconstruction of genre tropes, I began to realize that my study of film was affecting the way I thought about my own writing. Most of my recent nonfiction books, for example, tend to deploy a style that I informally call "smart self-help," which combines conventions from standard advice writing—a genre I was immersed in as a teenager and young adult, and for which I feel extreme affection—with more sophisticated forms from general nonfiction writing. Most books in these categories tend to fall into one bin or the other: you're either Stephen Covey or Malcolm Gladwell. I like to mix them. I hadn't thought much about this decision other than it's what felt natural to me. Studying Tarantino, however, I realized that working with lower genre tropes when pursuing higher ends, if given the right formal attention, can be a powerful creative exercise. Film has nothing to do with my writing career, but studying film enlarged my ambitions as an author.

There's nothing special about cinema in this case study. The bigger observation is that there can be utility in immersing yourself in appreciation for fields that are *different* from your own. It can be daunting to directly study great work in your profession, as you already know too much about it. Confronting the gap between what the masters produce and your current capabilities is disheartening. When you study an unrelated field, the pressure is reduced, and you can approach the topic with a more playful openness. When I read great nonfiction writers, I often find myself white-knuckling the book, trying to figure out what they're doing that I'm not. This is useful, but also exhausting. When I'm studying a great film, by contrast, I can just enjoy it without reservation, and in doing so find a refreshing jolt of inspiration. Consider this on your own journey toward developing an obsession with quality. Understand your own field, to be sure, but also focus on what's great about other domains. It's here that you can find a more flexible source of inspiration, a reminder of what makes the act of creation so exciting in the first place.

START YOUR OWN INKLINGS

In the mid-1930s, C. S. Lewis, then a professor of English literature at Magdalen College at Oxford University, started an informal writing and discussion club. He invited his friends to attend, including, notably, J. R. R. Tolkien, also a professor at Oxford at the time. At first, they met every week or so at Lewis's rooms at Magdalen, where they would read works in progress and discuss their literary ambitions. They later added the tradition of meeting one morning a week for a beer and discussion at the Eagle and Child, a pub in the center of Oxford. They called themselves the Inklings.

It was in these meetings that Lewis began his interest in writing speculative fiction. In 1938, drawing on the encouragement and guidance of the group, he published *Out of the Silent Planet*, a space travel story that attempted to correct some of the dehumanizing trends that he and Tolkien had observed in early science fiction writing of the period. This was the first in a trilogy of novels that laid the foundation for him to shift his fiction ambitions toward the world of fantasy, leading eventually to the Chronicles of Narnia series. Tolkien, for his part, drew heavily on feedback from the group to help shape the growing collection of connected fictional mythologies that would, later in his life, evolve into *The Lord of the Rings*. Indeed, Tolkien biographer Raymond Edwards describes the Inklings as a "partial midwife" for Tolkien's fantasy masterwork.

Later commentators would describe the Inklings as coming together for the specific mission of rejecting modernism and introducing fantastical narrative forms that could make Christian morality more accessible. But as Edwards argues, such analysis was both "over-solemn" and "exaggerated." As he elaborates, "The Inklings was, above all else, a collection of Lewis's friends. . . . Like most 'writers' groups, their main function was as an audience, to listen and criticize and encourage." It's here that we find the exportable lesson of the Inklings. When you gather with other people who share similar professional ambitions, the collective taste of the group can be superior to that of any individual. This follows, in part, from the diversity of approaches that people take toward creation in a given field. When you combine the opinions of multiple practitioners of your craft, more possibilities and nuance emerge. There's also a focusing effect that comes from performing for a crowd. When you want to impress other people, or add to the conversations in a meaningful way, your mind slips into a higher gear than what's easily accessible in solo introspection. Forming a group of like-minded professionals, all looking to improve what they're doing, provides a shortcut to improving your taste, an instantaneous upgrade to the standard of quality that you're pursuing.

BUY A FIFTY-DOLLAR NOTEBOOK

In the spring of 2010, early in my first year as a computer science postdoc, I decided on a whim to buy a high-end lab notebook I saw for sale at the MIT bookstore. It featured thick, acid-free, archival-quality paper printed with a light grid pattern and stamped with big black page numbers in the upper right corner. The notebook was held together with a durable double spiral and featured thick cardboard covers. Lab scientists take these notebooks seriously. The records of their experiments and results not only organize their work but also can be key evidence in patent disputes. (Alexander Graham Bell's carefully maintained lab notebooks, for example, played a critical role in his successful patent dispute with rival telephone inventor Elisha Gray.)

The trade-off for this increased quality is expense. Though I don't remember exactly how much I paid in 2010 for that notebook, I remember it was a lot for me at the time—probably somewhere around fifty dollars. This cost, however, was part of what attracted me to it. Knowing how much I had spent, I figured, would make me more careful about what I wrote on its archival-quality pages, which would force me to be more structured and careful in my thinking. This might sound like an odd gambit, but progress in theoretical computer science research often reduces to a game of cognitive chicken in which whoever is able to hold out longer through the mental discomfort of working through a proof element in their mind will end up with the sharper result. My biggest self-criticism as a researcher at the time was that I was bailing out too early when trying to think hard about a theorem or new algorithm. I hoped that a fancy notebook would keep me in the game a little longer.

I ended up using this notebook for a little more than two years, recording my final page of notes in December 2012—a period that spans my entire postdoc and my first year as an assistant professor. I know these precise dates because I recently found the notebook among a stack of old planners on a shelf toward the back of my bedroom closet. As I leafed through its pages, I was struck by how neatly I had inscribed my equations and diagrams. (In the cheaper notebooks I buy by the bushel, my scrawl is often barely legible.) Over that entire two-year period, I used only ninety-seven of the notebook's pages, filling each to its margins. Another thing that struck me was the familiarity of so many of the proof sketches and equations that made their way into the notebook. As I reviewed those ninety-seven pages, I found core results from what would become seven different peer-review publications, as well as the foundational thinking for what became my first major National Science Foundation grant as a young professor. This was one of many different notebooks I used during this short period of my academic career, but there's no doubt that this unusually expensive option played a disproportionate role in my productivity.

The general idea that quality tools can increase the quality of your work is not unique to my early academic career. Novelists find a burst of energy when they switch from a generic word processor to professional writing software like Scrivener, just as screenwriters feel more capable when they buy Final Draft to compose their movies. It's true that these more expensive tools include more features than their cheaper counterparts, but the "I'm a professional now" vibe they induce is arguably just as valuable. We see a similar effect in podcasters who buy the $300 Shure microphone famously used by Joe Rogan. In most cases, their audience wouldn't care about the minor quality difference between that professional mic and a cheaper USB option, but to the aspiring podcaster, it's a signal to themselves that they're taking the pursuit seriously. We also see these dynamics at play when computer programmers set up elaborate digital workstations featuring two or three monitors. These programmers will swear that the ability to see multiple windows at once increases productivity. This is true to an extent, but earlier generations of computer programmers seemed to be plenty productive before the recent introduction of graphic drivers capable of supporting multiple displays. Part of the power of these setups is found in their complexity, which puts the user in a specialized mindset, ready to do the hard work of writing efficient programs.

The pursuit of quality is not a casual endeavor. If you want your mind on board with your plans to evolve your abilities, then investing in your tools is a good way to start.

Interlude: What about Perfectionism?

When I was working on this chapter, I received a note from a professor named Meegan who was worried about my use of the phrase *obsess over quality*. She had recently completed and submitted the manuscript for a book that "took much too long to finish" because she had "internalized this notion that every aspect had to be perfect." Obsession, she pointed out, can be paralyzing. Quality matters, but if it becomes everything, you may never finish.

As we have throughout this book, we can find a nuanced take on this issue from the world of traditional knowledge workers. Let's turn our attention to popular music, and focus, in particular, on 1967: a year that changed this art form in profound but complicated ways. The seed of these transformations was planted in 1966, when the Beatles set off on a world tour just days after finishing their seventh studio album, *Revolver*. The plan was to start in West Germany before moving on to Tokyo, and then Manila. After a break, the tour would return to North America for an additional two weeks of performances, concluding with a final blowout concert at the cavernous Candlestick Park, in San Francisco.

Issues quickly mounted. In Japan, the tour promoter had struggled to find a venue big enough to seat the anticipated crowds. They settled on Nippon Budokan, a massive arena that had been originally built to house the judo competition during the 1964 Olympic Games in Tokyo. In Japan, however, judo is sacred, as was the location of the Budokan, in the imperial and spiritual center of the city, adjacent to the emperor's palace. To quote Clifford Williamson, a historian who wrote a 2017 article on the Beatles' 1966 tour, the fact that a Western pop group was going to perform in such a charged setting created a "major backlash." The Japanese prime minister expressed "discomfort," as did several important media figures. Threats from extremist groups such as the Greater Japan Patriotic Party were sufficiently dire that the Beatles debated whether they should scrap the show and avoid the country completely. In the end, more than thirty-five thousand police were mobilized to help ensure their safety.

The next tour stop, Manila, the capital of the Philippines, should have been easier. But it wasn't. "From the moment we landed it was bad news," George Harrison would later recall. In the lead-up to the visit, Imelda Marcos, wife to the Philippines' kleptocratic president, Ferdinand Marcos, delivered an invitation for the Beatles to attend a reception at the presidential palace. Following the band's standard rule to avoid diplomatic events, the Beatles' manager, Brian Epstein, turned her down. As Williamson explains, this was a mistake. Imelda's request wasn't an invitation, it was "a summons." The Filipino press covered the slight, televising empty tables and crying children at the reception. Imelda professed she preferred the Rolling Stones. More backlash ensued, and the Beatles soon faced a barrage of petty acts of revenge. Room service calls at their hotel were ignored. The promised support staff to help move the band's equipment disappeared. Escalators were turned off at the national airport to force the band to walk upstairs with their gear as they hastened to leave the country.

The Beatles' subsequent return to North America offered little relief from controversy. Earlier in 1966, John Lennon had conducted an interview with the *Evening Standard*. The profile was unremarkable, but hidden among bored banalities was the following provocative quip: "Christianity will go, it will vanish and shrink. . . . We're more popular than Jesus now." In the UK, the statement went unnoticed, but right around the time the band was arriving in the US for the final leg of their 1966 tour, a teen magazine named *Datebook* reproduced the interview, drawing attention to his quote about Jesus. The blowback in the American South was fierce. Boycotts were organized and Beatles albums were burned. The Ku Klux Klan threatened violence. Once again, the band members found themselves considering whether they should cancel appearances, and Lennon had to release an apology statement. In August, the Beatles finally made it to San Francisco for their final performance of the tour. As the band was traveling to Candlestick Park for the show, exhausted from the controversies of the preceding months, not to mention the general fatigue of having recorded and promoted seven albums in three years, John, Paul, George, and Ringo made a fateful decision: They were done with touring. For good.

It was this decision by the Beatles to stop performing that ended up transforming pop music the next year, in 1967. Three months had passed since their performance in San Francisco, and now, rested and resolved, the band gathered at EMI Studios in London to record a new type of pop album. Without the need to perform their songs in arenas and theaters, they were free to experiment. "With the producer George Martin aiding and abetting them," explains the *New York Times* music critic Jon Pareles, "the Beatles insisted on sonic abstractions, dropping the realistic illusions of most studio recording and distorting and manipulating sounds in ways that would be all but impossible to reproduce on stage."

The band manipulated tape speeds and overlaid different musical styles onto the same track. They integrated Indian instruments that George Harrison had learned under the tutelage of Ravi Shankar, including the sitar, tamboura, and swarmandal, and hired classical musicians to play string and horn accompaniments. They ended up spending around seven hundred hours in the studio, spread over one hundred twenty-nine days. (To understand how extravagant such a lengthy recording process was at the time, keep in mind that the first Beatles album, *Please Please Me*, released four years earlier in 1963, was recorded in a single day, requiring less than seven hundred *minutes* of total studio time.) The result of all of these creative and painstaking efforts was twelve tracks, spanning a little more than half an hour, representing one of the first commercial concept albums in the history of popular music. The Beatles titled it *Sgt. Pepper's Lonely Hearts Club Band*. It would go on to sell 2.5 million copies during its first three months and reach the number one spot on the Billboard charts, where it remained for three months, the longest stay at the top spot for any Beatles album. Perhaps more important, it almost single-handedly destroyed the long-dominant culture of pop song singles and hit parade charts. It made the album the defining artistic output of the popular music scene and ushered in a new era of progressive music and sonic experimentation.

The freedom of pop music from the constraints of performability, however, soon proved a double-edged sword. As Pareles elaborates, even though the Beatles' eighth release was a triumph, "critics vilify 'Sgt. Pepper' as the album that brought lonely perfectionism to rock recording." More bands retreated into studios to tinker with knobs and electronics in an attempt to find new experimental styles. In this long and slow quest for perfection, a lot of the immediacy and energy of rock was leached from the genre as musicians became lost in their own heads. The results were often disappointing. "For every genuine fusion . . . there were a dozen schlock hybrids," writes Pareles.

As Meegan correctly pointed out: this danger of creative perfectionism looms over this final principle of slow productivity. To obsess over quality is to become the Beatles in 1967, walking into EMI Studios with no limits on how long you can spend experimenting with your sitars and multitrack tape machines. To walk out one hundred twenty-nine days later with *Sgt. Pepper* requires you to traverse a razor's edge. Obsession requires you to get lost in your head, convinced that you can do just a little bit better given some more time. Greatness requires the ability to subsequently pull yourself out of your self-critical reverie before it's too late. The reason I dwell on the Beatles in this example is that they provide both a warning about the perfectionism that accompanies obsession and a canonical example of what it looks like to defeat this foe.

The band may have spent many more hours than they ever had before recording *Sgt. Pepper*, but their available time wasn't unlimited. Once their sessions began making progress, the Beatles' music publisher, EMI, released two singles, creating urgency to complete the project. The group also placed their efforts into a longer-term vision. Their 1965 album *Rubber Soul* had inspired Brian Wilson's innovative *Pet Sounds*, which Paul McCartney later cited as the primary influence on *Sgt. Pepper*. When your output is only one step among many on a collaborative path toward creative progress, the pressure to get everything just right is reduced. Your goal is instead reduced to knocking the metaphorical ball back over the net with enough force for the game to proceed. Here we find as good a general strategy for balancing obsession and perfectionism as I've seen: Give yourself enough time to produce something great, but not unlimited time. Focus on creating something good enough to catch the attention of those whose taste you care about, but relieve yourself of the need to forge a masterpiece. Progress is what matters. Not perfection.

Proposition: Bet on Yourself

Jewel wasn't the only breakout musician of the 1990s to take risks early in her career. Most people first learned about Alanis Morissette when her 1995 album, *Jagged Little Pill*, surged to sell over thirty-three million copies and win five Grammys, including Album of the Year. This may have been Morissette's first American record, but it was far from her introduction to the entertainment industry. While still a child, Morissette made her acting debut on Nickelodeon's cult sketch show *You Can't Do That on Television*, and her public singing debut with a performance on *Star Search* (she lost in the first round). In 1989, at the age of fifteen, she recorded a demo tape with the help of a Canadian rock band called the Stampeders. This led to a deal with the Canadian division of MCA. Her first album, *Alanis*, which featured highly produced dance pop, went platinum after its release in Canada in 1991. Her perky stage presence and big hair inspired comparisons to the 1980's pop sensation Debbie Gibson.

Morissette, however, didn't like the comparisons to Gibson, as she felt she was capable of more serious work. Though she would have likely enjoyed continued success had she continued with the pop style featured in *Alanis*, for her next album, *Now Is the Time*, Morissette instead turned her attention to less-produced ballads built on more personal lyrics—a style that she felt was capable of pushing her to the next level of her career.* This second record sold only half the number of copies as her first, leading her record label to drop her. But Morissette kept pushing. With the help of her music publisher, copies of her first two albums made their way to the New York–based manager Scott Welch. He heard something special in Morissette's voice, but agreed that the pop style wasn't sustainable. Welch arranged for Morissette to travel to Los Angeles to record a song with Glen Ballard, a veteran scribe known for cowriting Michael Jackson's "Man in the Mirror" and Wilson Phillips's "Hold On." The plan was to record a single track in Ballard's home studio. Instead, over a period of twenty inspired sessions, they recorded twenty songs. As Ballard later recalled about working with Morissette:

> She just wanted to be an *artist*. She didn't want the system to tell her they "didn't need her anymore." She just wanted to say what she felt. . . . She just wanted to write songs and express herself.

---

* As hinted in the 2021 documentary about Morissette, *Jagged*, her push for independence and exploration of more complicated themes in her music was motivated in part by some abuses she encountered as a young woman in the entertainment industry.

Those sessions included demos of almost every track that would end up on *Jagged Little Pill*. The combination of Morissette's powerful, raw voice with her cutting lyrics proved perfect for a moment when alternative music was ascendant. The album began with a modest release from Maverick Records, a boutique label co-owned by Madonna, but when Los Angeles's influential KROQ radio station started playing "You Oughta Know," its switchboards were flooded with requests. When it added "Hand in My Pocket" to the rotation a few weeks later, stations from around the country followed its lead. The album took off, creating what Ballard later described as "a firestorm."

Morissette's decision to walk away from upbeat pop shares obvious similarities with Jewel's decision to turn down a million-dollar record deal—both artists were willing to take risks in pursuit of a larger goal. The details of these decisions, however, differ in subtle but important ways. Jewel turned down the big money because she knew she needed more time to develop herself into a professional musician. This personifies my earlier claim that quality requires you to slow down. Morissette, by contrast, was already a successful professional musician when she left pop. Her change was instead a high-stakes bet on her ability to be even better. Losing her record deal was scary, but this fear provided her the drive needed to push her abilities to the point where she was able to create something miraculous during those epic recording sessions in Glen Ballard's home studio.

This proposition argues that betting on yourself in this manner—with nontrivial stakes for failure but attractive rewards for success—is a good general strategy for pushing the quality of your work to a new level. Nothing about this idea, of course, is specific to the music industry. One of the more famous examples of a self-bet in recent history comes from the world of business: Bill Gates dropping out of Harvard in 1975 to start Microsoft. Today, we're used to the idea of precocious tech types leaving college to start software companies, but this wasn't a thing back then. When Gates left Harvard, there was no software industry (he created it), and the personal computers that he saw as the future were still available only as a hobby kit that interfaced with its user through switches and blinking lights. The stakes for failure were high for Gates as he left Harvard, but this helped push him to do something spectacular.

Betting on yourself need not be as dramatic as losing a record deal or walking away from an Ivy League school. Simply by placing yourself in a situation where there exists pressure to succeed, even if moderate, can provide an important accelerant in your quest for quality. In the advice that follows, you'll encounter multiple approaches for integrating reasonable pressure of this type into your professional life. The goal in betting on yourself, as you'll see, is to push yourself to a new level without accidentally also pushing yourself into an unnaturally busy workload.

WRITE AFTER THE KIDS GO TO BED

Stephenie Meyer got the idea for *Twilight* from a dream in the summer of 2003. The experience was so vivid that she committed to doing whatever it would take to turn this seed of a concept into a fully realized book. At the time, however, she was a stay-at-home parent to three young boys, meaning that she would need to get creative with her writing schedule. As she explained:

> From that point on, not one day passed that I did not write *something*. On bad days, I would only type out a page or two; on good days, I would finish a chapter and then some. I mostly wrote at night, after the kids were asleep so that I could concentrate for longer than five minutes without being interrupted.

The story of a famous author getting their start scribbling after bedtime is not unique to Meyer. Clive Cussler started writing adventure novels in 1965. At the time, he was in his midthirties, working at a small advertising firm he cofounded in Newport Beach, California, when his wife took a job that required her to work night shifts. This left Cussler with nothing to do after he put his three kids to bed. Inspired by the recent success of Ian Fleming's James Bond novels, he decided to try adventure writing to fill the lonely hours. Tens of millions of copies sold later, Cussler, who died in 2020, clearly made the right bet.

The need to work on a passion project after hours, of course, is not unique to parents. During his final year at Harvard Medical School, for example, Michael Crichton knew he didn't plan to practice medicine after earning his degree. As reported in a 1970 *New York Times* profile of the author, who was then only twenty-seven years old, Crichton approached the dean to ask if he could spend his last semester at Harvard gathering information for a nonfiction book on medicine he planned to write. "Why should I spend the last half of my last year at medical school learning to read electrocardiograms when I never intended to practice?" he asked. The dean warned Crichton that writing a book wasn't easy. It was at this point that Crichton revealed that during his time at Harvard, he'd already written five books under pen names, and had at least two more underway. He would bring his portable typewriter with him to fill spare moments writing, including during vacations or while attending course lectures that failed to keep his attention. "Anyone who wanted to look at my transcript . . . could see when I was working on a book," he admitted.

John Grisham, who spent the 1990s battling with Crichton for bestseller-list supremacy, also got started in writing by sacrificing his free time. He began crafting his first novel, *A Time to Kill*, as a small-town lawyer with a seat in the Mississippi legislature. He worked on the manuscript early in the morning and in between meetings and court hearings. It took Grisham three years of these part-time efforts to finish the book. Before it was even published, he began working on his second. His plan all along was to write two books, and to keep going only if at least one of the two succeeded. This strategy turned out to be a good one. *A Time to Kill* flopped when it was first released. Fortunately for Grisham, his second book, *The Firm*, sold seven million copies.

These authors demonstrate one of the more approachable strategies for betting on yourself: temporarily dedicating significant amounts of free time to the project in question. The stakes here are modest: If you fail to reach the quality level that you seek, the main consequence is that during a limited period you've lost time you could have dedicated to more rewarding (or restful) activities. But this cost is sufficiently annoying to motivate increased attention toward your efforts. For a young Stephenie Meyer, for example, it likely wasn't fun to squeeze so much writing in between kid activities or into tired stretches late at night. Given the sacrifices this goal demanded, she was motivated to not waste time on a half-hearted effort. Determined to see her project through to the end, Meyer wrote every day, even if she completed only a few pages. (By contrast, I've seen more than a few academics or journalists, given a luxurious sabbatical to do nothing but write, struggle to make meaningful progress amid all their newfound freedom.)

This spare time strategy, of course, is not a sustainable way to work in the long term. Sacrificing too many of your leisure hours to extra work can violate *both* of the first two principles of slow productivity. But when deployed in moderation, dedicated to a specific project for a temporary period, this act of giving up something meaningful in pursuit of higher quality can become an effective bet on yourself. Meyer, for example, worked with intense focus for six months, but at the end of that tiring period, she ended up with an attention-catching manuscript. Little, Brown and Company soon offered her a $750,000 book deal.

REDUCE YOUR SALARY

Committing your free time to a project is one of the easier ways to bet on yourself. A more drastic option is to rely on the project for income. Few forces induce more focus than the need to pay bills. It's here, however, that we wander into some potentially dangerous territory. In American culture, there's a romantic appeal to the idea of quitting your stultifying job to pursuing a grander dream. Consider the writer examples from the preceding strategy: Clive Cussler ended up walking away from the ad agency he cofounded, while John Grisham abandoned a promising political career and law practice. There's immense appeal in the possibilities of dramatically upending your professional situation, as it feels like you might, in one grand move, dispatch all that you dislike about your current grind.

The problem, of course, is that for every Grisham there are a dozen other aspiring writers—or entrepreneurs, or artists—who end up slinking back to their old jobs, chastened and deeper in debt than when they started. It's hard to predict, in other words, whether your idea for a thriller will be more *A Time to Kill* or *The Firm*. Fortunately, we can find wisdom for navigating these challenges from the same literary examples we just cited. If you look closer at the career transitions of these bestselling writers, a more nuanced story emerges. As revealed in the obituaries that followed his death in 2020, for example, the path Cussler took from advertising to adventure novels was longer than what's implied by the well-worn tale of his conjuring the character of Dirk Pitt at night while his wife worked the late shift.

As previously noted, when Cussler began working on novels, he co-owned an advertising agency in Newport Beach. He wrote two manuscripts while living in California, *Pacific Vortex!* and *The Mediterranean Caper*, neither of which attracted interest from publishers. Cussler then moved to Denver to take a job with a larger agency. It was at this point that he developed a ruse to try to get attention for his languishing novels. He created a fake letterhead for an agency that didn't exist, and then sent a note to a real agent, Peter Lampack, asking if he was interested in taking on this promising new writer named Clive whom he didn't have time to represent. The plan worked, and *The Mediterranean Caper* was finally published in 1973. Cussler, however, still didn't leave advertising to write full time. He waited until 1975, after he sold his second book, *Iceberg*. Similar care can be found in the stories of our other examples. When Crichton left medicine, he had already published (many) books, some of which were bestsellers. Grisham didn't stop practicing law until Paramount unexpectedly bid $600,000 for the movie rights for *The Firm*.

It's in these details that we find a balanced strategy. Don't haphazardly quit your job to pursue a more meaningful project. Wait instead to make a major change until you have concrete evidence that your new interest satisfies the following two properties: first, people are willing to give you money for it, and second, you can replicate the result. In the context of writing, this might mean you've sold multiple books and proven there's a robust audience for your characters. In entrepreneurship, by contrast, this might mean that your side hustle generates a steady stream of sales. Once you've passed these thresholds, however, take action. This doesn't necessarily mean quitting your current job completely. It might instead mean that you reduce your hours, or take an unpaid leave. The key is to harness the stark motivation generated by the need for a pursuit to really work out. Clive Cussler completed four manuscripts before quitting his job as an advertising executive. But it was Cussler's fifth book, 1976's *Raise the Titanic!*, that finally broke through the noise and emerged as his first blockbuster bestseller.

ANNOUNCE A SCHEDULE

Dedicating time or sacrificing money for a project are two obvious bets to push you toward higher-quality work. A natural third option is to leverage your social capital. If you announce your work in advance to people you know, you'll have created expectations. If you fail to produce something notable, you'll pay a social cost in terms of embarrassment. Not surprisingly, this, too, can act as a powerful motivator.

The small town where I live right outside Washington, DC, is known for its arts culture. As a result, it's common to see flyers or receive emails about art shows of various types. Around the time I was writing this chapter, for example, two artisans on my street— a jewelry designer and a mixed-media painter—had recently announced an art market to be held over three successive weekends in a former commercial building that was in between tenants. They teamed up with a small-press printer who was creating attention-catching advertising hung throughout the neighborhood. These artists were now committed to producing the best work they could, as they'd soon have a large audience of their peers to impress.

This strategy of announcing a schedule to inspire quality works at different scales. It could be as small as an aspiring screenwriter setting up a date with a cinema-savvy friend to read through the first draft of a script. Or something as large as an entrepreneur publicizing a release date for a new product. There are few things we value more than the esteem of our fellow humans. Announcing a schedule for your work hijacks this quirk of our species' evolution to sharpen our focus on producing the best work possible.

ATTRACT AN INVESTOR

In 1977, a twenty-nine-year-old director named John Carpenter was in England to screen his low-budget action film, *Assault on Precinct 13*, at the London Film Festival. The movie was too small for a wide theatrical release, and it hadn't made much money in the few places where it was shown, but its director flashed talent. "[The film] is one of the most powerful and exciting crime thrillers from a new director in a long time," wrote Ken Wlaschin, the London Film Festival's director. "It grabs hold of the audience and simply doesn't let go." It was there in London that Carpenter was introduced to a financier named Moustapha Akkad, who was looking to invest in American mainstream movies. Akkad had around $300,000 left over from another project, *Lion of the Desert*, and the young director, along with his producing partner Irwin Yablans, pushed Akkad to invest these extra funds in a new idea they'd been discussing for a horror film about a killer stalking babysitters. "We basically shamed Moustapha into it," Yablans later recalled. "I told him, '$300,000 is probably too much for you to invest,' knowing he couldn't back off because of his pride."

Akkad was intrigued by a pitch in which Carpenter walked him through his vision of the film scene by scene. The deal was sealed when the director agreed to not take fees, instead betting his remuneration on the movie finding success with audiences. This turned out to be a good bet. After a tight twenty-one-day shooting schedule in the spring of 1978, the movie was finished, and its original working title of *The Babysitter Murders* was changed to that more evocative *Halloween*. The film went on to gross over $45 million, making it, at the time, the most successful independent film in history. It also set the standard for the horror movie genre for decades to follow and launched Carpenter's career.

Assault on Precinct 13 is a cool film, but *Halloween* is great. The difference was the scale of investment supporting Carpenter. The easy explanation for this observation is that more money enables better production quality. This is partially true. Carpenter, along with his then unknown director of photography, Dean Cundey, spent nearly half of Akkad's $300,000 on brand-new, lightweight Panavision cameras—a new technology at the time that allowed them to film in long, gliding Steadicam shots while maintaining a cinematic aspect ratio. (Cundey took particular advantage of the wide-screen format, which allowed multiple elements to be integrated into the same visual scene, to create some iconic scares.) But the fancy cameras alone don't explain the movie's success. The pressure and drive to satisfy Akkad, who had invested serious money in the project, helped push Carpenter's craftsmanship to new levels. His goal with *Assault* was to showcase his talents. His goal with *Halloween* was to create a classic movie. This is an important difference.

This same lesson applies to other endeavors. When someone has invested in your project, you'll experience amplified motivation to pay back their trust. This is true for investments of financial capital, as with Carpenter and Akkad. But it's also true for investments of sweat equity, such as when a friend helps you build the sets for a theatrical production or spends an afternoon stuffing envelopes for a marketing campaign for your new business. Attracting other people to invest in you and your idea is a dramatic bet on yourself and your ability to not let others down. In the drive to avoid this disappointment, greatness can be found.

CONCLUSION

I opened this book with the story of a young John McPhee lying on a picnic table in his backyard, looking up at an ash tree, trying to make sense of a complicated article he was struggling to write. As McPhee's career advanced, he evolved, through trial and error, a more involved and repeatable process for producing his distinctive style of long-form journalism. As he explained in *Draft No. 4*, he would begin by copying all of his observations from his notebooks, and transcribing all of his tape-recorded interviews, onto fresh pages, pounded out on an Underwood 5 manual typewriter. "The note-typing could take many weeks," he explains, "but it collected everything in one legible place, and it ran all the raw material in some concentration through the mind."

Once he completed this step, McPhee would be confronted with a stack of neatly typed pages, many containing multiple unrelated scraps of thoughts or observations, separated by a few lines of white space. To make sense of this collection, he would code each section with a short description in the margin, indicating the relevant *story component* it covered. A standard long-form article might include notes on around thirty different components. *Encounters with the Archdruid*, McPhee's epic two-part profile of the environmentalist David Brower, required thirty-six.

McPhee would photocopy these pages, and then use a pair of scissors to cut out each self-contained chunk of notes into its own "sliver" of paper. (When McPhee eventually bought a personal computer in the 1980s and began using an electronic system to organize his notes, he referred to the machine as a "five-thousand-dollar pair of scissors.") Each sliver was placed in a plain manila folder that corresponded to its story component. The result was a stack of folders, each dedicated to a single subject, filled with scraps of paper that collectively contained every relevant fact, quote, or observation.

Next, McPhee would label a three-by-five index card for each of these story components, and spread them on a sheet of plywood propped up between two sawhorses—"an essential part of my office furniture in those years"—so he could physically move them around in search of a workable structure for his story. Sometimes the right conceptual architecture would come to him in just a few hours. Sometimes he had to let the board sit there for days, returning to it occasionally. There was no rushing this stage of the process: he couldn't write until the order of cards made sense.

Once McPhee was finally pleased with his structure, he could turn, at long last, to putting words on the page. When writing, he would deal with one story component at a time, tackling them in the order in which they were arranged on the plywood sheet. When writing about a specific component, he would remove all the relevant slivers of notes from the corresponding folder and lay them out ladderlike on a card table set up next to his Underwood 5. "The procedure eliminated nearly all distraction and concentrated just the material I had to deal with in a given day or week," McPhee explains. "It painted me into a corner, yes, but in doing so it freed me to write."

There's a reason why I opened and closed our exploration of slow productivity with two different stories about John McPhee. When we encountered the initial tale of McPhee under the ash tree, in the very first pages of this book, the idea of a slower notion of productivity was more an intuition or vague aspiration than something concrete and widely adoptable. McPhee's languid focus under that tree seemed to resonate with the average burned-out knowledge worker, but how exactly one might translate that resonance into practical action was still hazy. We opened on a feeling, but needed a plan.

By the time we've arrived at this second, more detailed story of John McPhee, five long chapters later, the contours of such a plan have hopefully become apparent. In those preceding pages, I detailed how the knowledge sector derailed from reasonable notions of organizing work, and then walked you through three principles for systematically cultivating something better—a philosophy I called slow productivity. This was not meant as a reactionary response to our current moment of overload, but instead a game plan for a viable replacement. It's this practicality that I hoped to capture in the second tale of McPhee. In his careful and deliberate process of typing out his notes and slicing them into slivers, and then organizing index cards on a plywood board and arranging material ladderlike on a card table, we see the promise introduced under McPhee's backyard ash tree transformed into something more systematic. Slowing down isn't about protesting work. It's instead about finding a better way to do it.

I have two goals for this book. The first is focused: to help as many people as possible free themselves from the dehumanizing grip of pseudo-productivity. As I noted in the introduction, not everyone has access to this outcome. The philosophy I developed is meant primarily for those who engage in skilled labor with significant amounts of autonomy. This target audience covers large swaths of the knowledge sector, including most freelancers, solopreneurs, and small-business owners, as well as those in fields like academia, where great freedom is afforded in how you choose and organize your efforts.

If you fall into one of these categories, and are exhausted by the chronic overload and fast pacing of pseudo-productivity, then I urge you to consider radically transforming your professional life along the three principles I proposed. Do fewer things. Work at a natural pace. Obsess over quality. Depending on the details of your role, this probably won't mean spending weeks staring up at tree branches or typing notes on a typewriter, but it will almost certainly lead to a more sustainable relationship with your job.*

---

* For the freelance writers among my readers, I recommend the following essay about McPhee, which argues that the changing economics of publishing have made his slower focus on long-form articles hard to replicate: Malcolm Harris, "Who Can

My second goal for this book applies more broadly. Slow productivity is just one response among many to a much bigger problem: The world of cognitive work lacks coherent ideas about how our efforts should be organized and measured. Using visible activity as a proxy for useful labor was at best a temporary fix, slapped together in the mid-twentieth century as managers struggled to reorient themselves amid the sudden emergence of a new economic sector. As I detailed in part 1, this managerial Band-Aid has long since come loose. Pseudo-productivity began to spiral toward unsustainability once the front office IT revolution made endless work available and removed any natural restrictions on the pace of these efforts. The additional disruptions introduced by the pandemic provided the final acceleration needed for this rotation to shatter the whole system into pieces. There's a reason why it's now so common to encounter critics who promote an exhausted nihilism in which overload and misery are an inescapable fate. The way we're working no longer works.

What's needed is more intentional thinking about what we mean by "productivity" in the knowledge sector—seeking ideas that start from the premise that these efforts must be sustainable

---

Afford to Write Like John McPhee?," *New Republic*, September 13, 2017, newrepublic.com/article/144795/can-afford-write-like-john-mcphee. The reality here is somewhat more complicated. While it's true that magazines aren't going to pay you a good salary to write one forty-thousand-word article every two years, it's important to also note that McPhee makes it clear in *Draft No. 4* that being a "staff writer" for *The New Yorker* in the 1960s was a meaningless title (basically, it just meant you were a freelancer they liked to work with) and that he didn't make a ton of money from articles alone. To make ends meet required the success of his books and his position teaching writing at Princeton. The bigger point behind the McPhee story, however, is not the details of how he writes magazine articles, but the idea that productivity at the large scale doesn't require frantic busyness at the small.

and engaging for the actual humans doing the work. Slow productivity is one example of this thinking, but it shouldn't be the only one. My long-term wish is that this movement kicks off many others, creating a marketplace of different concepts of productivity, each of which might apply to different types of workers or sensibilities. Slow productivity, for example, is designed to be actionable, providing ideas that individuals can implement immediately. But it would be good to balance this approach with some that more ambitiously seek to rework how organizations are managed, or even the legislation that constrains how our market economy operates. Revolution requires rebellions of many different scopes, from the practical and immediate to the fiery and ideological.

Regardless of the details of how we make progress, it's hard to overemphasize the importance of these general efforts. There's a reason why in the title of his influential 1999 paper, Peter Drucker labeled knowledge worker productivity as "the biggest challenge." Getting this right could drastically improve the lives of millions.

Toward the end of a wide-ranging 2010 interview with *The Paris Review*, John McPhee marveled at the idea that anyone might think of him as being unusually hardworking:

> And if somebody says to me, "You're a prolific writer"—it seems so odd. It's like the difference between geological time and human time. On a certain scale, it does look like I do a lot. But that's my day, all day long, sitting there wondering when I'm going to be able to get started. And the routine of

doing this six days a week puts a little drop in a bucket each day, and that's the key. Because if you put a drop in a bucket every day, after three hundred and sixty-five days, the bucket's going to have some water in it.

Slow productivity, more than anything else, is a plea to step back from the frenzied activity of the daily grind. It's not that these efforts are arbitrary: our anxious days include tasks and appointments that really do need to get done. But once you realize, as McPhee did, that this exhausted scrambling is often orthogonal to the activities that matter, your perspective changes. A slower approach to work is not only feasible, but is likely superior to the ad hoc pseudo-productivity that dictates the professional lives of so many today. If you collect modest drops of meaningful effort for 365 days, McPhee reminds us, you'll end the year with a bucket that's pretty damn full. This is what ultimately matters: where you end up, not the speed at which you get there, or the number of people you impress with your jittery busyness along the way.

We've tried the fast approach for at least the past seventy years. It isn't working. The time has come to try something slower.

ACKNOWLEDGMENTS

I cannot pinpoint the exact moment at which the phrase *slow productivity* entered my lexicon. The philosophy seems to have emerged somewhat spontaneously during the first year of the coronavirus pandemic, a period in which I began an intense and immensely fruitful dialogue about work, productivity, and meaning with my audience. I want to thank them first and foremost for their essential role in pushing me and my thinking forward.

Once these ideas were formed, it was then my literary agent, Laurie Abkemeier, who helped me organize them into a coherent book project. It was during this process that Laurie and I passed the milestone of having worked together for more than two decades, a professional relationship and friendship that reaches all the way back to a twenty-year-old version of myself, then a rising senior at Dartmouth, looking for representation to sell a book about succeeding in college. It's hard to overemphasize the impact that Laurie and her mentorship have had in shaping all aspects of my professional writing career. For this, I am immensely thankful.

I must also thank, of course, the team at Portfolio Books, under the leadership of Adrian Zackheim, for continuing to believe in me and my ideas. This is the third book I've written for Portfolio, and the third book acquired and edited by Niki Papadopoulos, who has been an author's dream to work with over these past six or so years. I was also excited when Lydia Yadi, who had edited the UK editions of my recent books, joined the editorial team for *Slow Productivity*. I'm thankful for all of the incisive comments and suggestions she contributed to help whip this manuscript into shape.

Further appreciation must be given to the talented members of the Portfolio marketing and publicity team who have worked with me so successfully on my past projects, and with whom I look forward to collaborating on this new endeavor. This includes, notably, Margot Stamas, who has worked on all of my Portfolio titles to date, and Mary Kate Rogers, who has also been with me for multiple projects. They make the process of telling the world about my work both painless and exciting.

I also want to thank Josh Rothman and Mike Agger, my editors at *The New Yorker*, where many of the ideas in this book were initially developed. Their continued support of my writing and ideas has provided a critical engine to my growth as an author and thinker. I still remain awed and honored by the trust they've placed in me and the mentorship they've shared.

And finally, I must thank my indefatigable wife, Julie, for putting up with all the sacrifices involved in having a partner with a troubling addiction to writing books. She's known me for every one of the eight books I've published to date, so she knows all too well the demands of this process. For this understanding and patience, I remain, as always, deeply grateful.

NOTES

INTRODUCTION

1 **"I lay down on it"**: John McPhee, *Draft No. 4: On the Writing Process* (New York: Farrar, Straus and Giroux, 2018), 17.
1 **McPhee had already published**: In my count of five earlier reported articles, I am skipping the short Talk of the Town pieces, as well as an early short story he published in the magazine. McPhee's *New Yorker* archive can be accessed at newyorker.com/contributors/john-mcphee. The precise dating of McPhee's stint at *Time* comes from Jeffrey Somers, "Jon McPhee: His Life and Work," ThoughtCo., July 20, 2019, thoughtco.com/john-mcphee-biography-4153952.
1 **McPhee had previously written profiles**: John McPhee, "A Sense of Where You Are," *New Yorker*, January 23, 1965, newyorker.com/magazine/1965/01/23/a-sense-of-where-you-are.
1 **He had also written historical**: John McPhee, "A Reporter at Large: Oranges—I," *New Yorker*, May 7, 1966, newyorker.com/magazine/1966/05/07/oranges-2; and John McPhee, "A Reporter at Large: Oranges—II," *New Yorker*, May 14, 1966, newyorker.com/magazine/1966/05/14/oranges-3.
2 **McPhee spent eight months**: McPhee, *Draft No. 4*, 17.
2 **"To lack confidence"**: McPhee, *Draft No. 4*, 19.
2 **McPhee had met Brown**: McPhee, *Draft No. 4*, 19.
5 **"We are overworked"**: Celeste Headlee, *Do Nothing: How to Break Away from Overdoing, Overworking, and Underliving* (New York: Harmony Books, 2020), ix.

CHAPTER 1: THE RISE AND FALL OF PSEUDO-PRODUCTIVITY

13 **"Unless anybody hasn't noticed"**: Bill Carter, *Desperate Networks* (New York: Broadway Books, 2006), 42.

15 **"work on the productivity"**: Peter F. Drucker, "Knowledge-Worker Productivity: The Biggest Challenge," *California Management Review* 41, no. 2 (Winter 1999): 83.

16 **"In most cases, people"**: Tom Davenport quotes come from a phone interview conducted in December 2019. Here's the original *New Yorker* article for which this interview was conducted: Cal Newport, "The Rise and Fall of Getting Things Done," *New Yorker*, November 17, 2020, newyorker.com/tech/annals-of-technology/the-rise-and-fall-of-getting-things-done.

17 **This in turn made many:** *Encyclopaedia Britannica Online*, "Norfolk Four-Course System," accessed August 18, 2023, britannica.com/topic/Norfolk-four-course-system.

18 **Assembly lines are dreary:** "Moving Assembly Line Debuts at Ford Factory," History, October 6, 2020, history.com/this-day-in-history/moving-assembly-line-at-ford.

18 **By the end of the decade:** G. N. Georgano, *Cars: Early and Vintage, 1886–1930* (London: Grange-Universal, 1985).

19 **the optimal shovel load:** For more on Taylor and shovels, see "Frederick Winslow Taylor, the Patron Saint of the Shovel," Mental Floss, April 27, 2015, mentalfloss.com/article/63341/frederick-winslow-taylor-patron-saint-shovel.

20 **"The knowledge worker cannot":** Peter F. Drucker, *The Effective Executive: The Definitive Guide to Getting Things Done* (New York: HarperCollins, 2006), 4.

23 **One particularly damning analysis:** Jory MacKay, "Communication Overload: Our Research Shows Most Workers Can't Go 6 Minutes without Checking Email or IM," *RescueTime* (blog), July 11, 2018, blog.rescuetime.com/communication-multitasking-switches.

23 **A recent study conducted:** Actual study (the "Methodology" section supports the claim that the survey participants are primarily from knowledge work): McKinsey & Company and Lean In, *Women in the Workplace: 2021*, 2022, wiw-report.s3.amazonaws.com/Women_in_the_Workplace_2021.pdf. For a good summary of the findings, see Eliana Dockterman, "42% of Women Say They Have Consistently Felt Burned Out at Work in 2021," *Time*, September 27, 2021, time.com/6101751/burnout-women-in-the-workplace-2021.

24 **"The intersection of work":** Jennifer Liu, "U.S. Workers Are among the Most Stressed in the World, New Gallup Report Finds," Make It, CNBC, June 15, 2021, cnbc.com/2021/06/15/gallup-us-workers-are-among-the-most-stressed-in-the-world.html.

26 **"he found himself asking God":** Carter, *Desperate Networks*, 119.

27 **"Oh, this is for sure a show":** Carter, *Desperate Networks*, 120.

27 **"Zuiker wove his pitch magic":** Carter, *Desperate Networks*, 121.

28 **"You guys have to dig":** Carter, *Desperate Networks*, 125.

28 **When combined with CBS's:** A representative article from this period about *CSI*'s key role in pushing CBS back into first place is: "2000–01 Ratings History," The TV Ratings Guide, August 15, 1991, thetvratingsguide.com/1991/08/2000-01-ratings-history.html.

CHAPTER 2: A SLOWER ALTERNATIVE

31 **"What disturbs us most":** Details of Italians' reactions to the proposed McDonald's come from this contemporaneous UPI story: John Phillips, "McDonald's Brings Americanization Fears to Rome," UPI, May 10, 1986, upi.com/Archives/1986/05/10/McDonalds-brings-Americanization-fears-to-Rome/6908516081600.

31 **manifesto defined its goals:** "Slow Food Manifesto," 1989, Slow Food, slowfood.com/filemanager/Convivium%20Leader%20Area/Manifesto_ENG.pdf. Versions of the "Slow Food Manifesto" in other languages are available here: "Key Documents," Slow Food, slowfood.com/about-us/key-documents.

32 **Campania region in southern Italy:** The Vesuvian apricot is discussed in Michael Pollan, "Cruising on the Ark of Taste," *Mother Jones*, May 1, 2003, archived at michaelpollan.com/articles-archive/cruising-on-the-ark-of-taste.

32 **Held biannually, the event:** For more on the Salone del Gusto and the cited numbers, see Mark Notaras, "Slow Food Movement Growing Fast," *Our World*, October 31, 2014, ourworld.unu.edu/en/slow-food-movement-growing-fast.

33 **"Those who suffer":** Pollan, "Cruising on the Ark."

34 **"a serious contribution":** Pollan, "Cruising on the Ark."

35 **More recently, the Slow Media:** For a good introduction to Slow Media, I recommend Jennifer Rauch's 2018 book on the topic: Jennifer Rauch, *Slow Media: Why "Slow" Is Satisfying, Sustainable, and Smart* (Oxford: Oxford University Press, 2018), global.oup.com/academic/product/slow-media-9780190641795.

35 **"But now it has become":** Carl Honoré, *In Praise of Slowness: Challenging the Cult of Speed* (New York: HarperOne, 2005), 86.

36 **"Stop treating us":** AppleTogether, "Thoughts on Office-Bound Work," appletogether.org/hotnews/thoughts-on-office-bound-work.html.

36 **A full year after Cook's:** Jane Thier, "Tim Cook Called Remote Work 'the Mother of All Experiments.' Now Apple Is Cracking Down on Employees Who Don't Come in 3 Days a Week, Report Says," *Fortune*, March 24, 2023, fortune.com/2023/03/24/remote-work-3-days-apple-discipline-terminates-tracks-tim-cook.

37 **"They're at the vanguard":** Cal Newport, "What Hunter-Gatherers Can Teach Us about the Frustrations of Modern Work," *New Yorker*, November 2, 2022, newyorker.com/culture/office-space/lessons-from-the-deep-history-of-work.

37 **As the BBC reported:** Alex Christian, "Four-Day Workweek Trial: The Firms Where It Didn't Work," BBC, March 20, 2023, bbc.com/worklife/article/20230319-four-day-workweek-trial-the-firms-where-it-didnt-work.

37 **Though his bill:** Gili Malinsky, "10 Companies Adopting a 4-Day Workweek That Are Hiring Right Now," Make It, CNBC, March 19, 2023, cnbc.com/2023/03/19/companies-with-a-four-day-workweek-that-are-hiring-right-now.html; and Ben Tobin, "Lowe's Started Offering a 4-Day Work Week after Complaints of a 'Chaotic' Scheduling System. Employees Say They Love It," *Business Insider*, March 28, 2023, businessinsider.com/lowes-workers-say-love-4-day-work-week-with-exceptions-2023-3.

40 **Consider Isaac Newton working:** Cal Newport, "Newton's Productive School Break," *Cal Newport* (blog), March 23, 2023, calnewport.com/blog/2020/03/23/newtons-productive-school-break; and Cal Newport, "The Stone Carver in an Age of Computer Screens," *Cal Newport* (blog), October 27, 2020, calnewport.com/blog/2020/10/27/the-stone-carver-in-an-age-of-computer-screens.

40 **As I'll elaborate later:** Cal Newport, "What If Remote Work Didn't Mean Working from Home?," *New Yorker*, May 21, 2021, newyorker.com/culture/cultural-comment/remote-work-not-from-home.

CHAPTER 3: DO FEWER THINGS

47 **The author's name was not:** Claire Tomalin, *Jane Austen: A Life* (New York: Vintage Books, 1999), 220.

47 **only forty-one years old:** Two additional Jane Austen novels, *Persuasion* and *Northanger Abbey*, were published after her death.

48 **In chapter 6 of this memoir:** James Edward Austen Leigh, *A Memoir of Jane Austen* (London: Richard Bentley and Son, 1871; Project Gutenberg, 2006), chap. 6, 102, gutenberg.org/files/17797/17797-h/17797-h.htm.

48 **It's retold in modern accounts:** Mason Currey, *Daily Rituals: How Artists Work* (New York: Knopf, 2013), 25–26.

50 **As Claire Tomalin explains:** Tomalin, *Jane Austen*, 87.

50 **"easing of all the work":** Tomalin, *Jane Austen*, 122.

50 **"abstract herself from the daily life":** Tomalin, *Jane Austen*, 170.

51 **"There were no dances":** Tomalin, *Jane Austen*, 214.

52 **"In this way she":** Tomalin, *Jane Austen*, 213.

55 **"I started then to actually work weekends":** Lananh Nguyen and Harry Wilson, "HSBC Manager Heart Attack Prompts Viral Post about Overwork," *Bloomberg*, April 21, 2021, bloomberg.com/news/articles/2021-04-21/hsbc-manager-s-heart-attack-prompts-viral-post-about-overwork#xj4y7vzkg. For those who do not use LinkedIn and therefore cannot access the original post, a reproduction of his six resolutions can be found here as well: Alema Ljuca, "Heart Attack Survivor Shares New Life Resolutions and It Goes Viral," *Medium*, June 16, 2021, medium.com/better-advice/heart-attack-survivor-shares-new-life-resolutions-from-his-hospital-bed-5c7fd1aab2d8.

55 **"The digital intensity":** *Work Trend Index Annual Report: The Next Great Disruption Is Hybrid Work—Are We Ready?*, Microsoft, March 22, 2021, microsoft.com/en-us/worklab/work-trend-index/hybrid-work.

58 **"and decisions start to drag":** Cal Newport, "Why Remote Work Is So Hard—and How It Can Be Fixed," *New Yorker*, May 26, 2020, newyorker.com/culture/annals-of-inquiry/can-remote-work-be-fixed.

66 **"Here was a problem":** Simon Singh, *Fermat's Enigma: The Epic Quest to Solve the World's Greatest Mathematical Problem* (New York: Anchor Books, 1997), 6.

67 "I was electrified": Singh, *Fermat's Enigma*, 205.
67 "Wiles abandoned any work": Singh, *Fermat's Enigma*, 207.
68 "This apparent productivity": Singh, *Fermat's Enigma*, 210.
71 "legacies from years": Jenny Blake, *Free Time* (Washington, DC: Ideapress, 2022), 7.
72 "To do real good physics": Here is an article from 2014 I wrote about the clip, including the identification of the excerpt cited here (the YouTube clip of the 1981 video has been taken down for copyright violation reasons): Cal Newport, "Richard Feynman Didn't Win a Nobel by Responding Promptly to E-mails," *Cal Newport* (blog), April 20, 2014, calnewport.com/blog/2014/04/20/richard-feynman-didnt-win-a-nobel-by-responding-promptly-to-e-mails. The second half of this quote can also be found in Feynman's *Los Angeles Times* obituary: Lee Dye, "Nobel Physicist R. P. Feynman of Caltech Dies," *Los Angeles Times*, February 16, 1988, latimes.com/archives/la-xpm-1988-02-16-mn-42968-story.html.
73 "Irresponsibility requires eternal vigilance": Lawrence Grobel, "The Remarkable Dr. Feynman: Caltech's Eccentric Richard P. Feynman Is a Nobel Laureate, a Member of the Shuttle Commission, and Arguably the World's Best Theoretical Physicist," *Los Angeles Times*, April 20, 1986, latimes.com/archives/la-xpm-1986-04-20-tm-1265-story.html. For a good, concise history of Feynman and the commission, including the detail of his former student roping him into participation, I recommend this article: Kevin Cook, "How Legendary Physicist Richard Feynman Helped Crack the Case on the Challenger Disaster," *Literary Hub*, June 9, 2021, lithub.com/how-legendary-physicist-richard-feynman-helped-crack-the-case-on-the-challenger-disaster.
76 "This industry, visible": Benjamin Franklin, *Autobiography of Benjamin Franklin*, ed. John Bigelow (Philadelphia: J. B. Lippincott, 1868; Project Gutenberg, 2006), chap. 6, https://www.gutenberg.org/ebooks/20203.
77 daily checklist of cardinal virtues: Franklin, *Autobiography*, chap. 9.
77 "Part of Franklin's problem": H. W. Brands, *The First American: The Life and Times of Benjamin Franklin* (New York: Anchor Books, 2002), 164.
78 "Hall became Franklin's foreman": Brands, *The First American*, 166.
79 "I am settling my old": Brands, *The First American*, 189–90 (emphasis mine).
80 Soon after, in part owing: Brands, *The First American*, 200–205.
81 "When I go up north": Ian Rankin, "Ian Rankin: 'Solitude, Coffee, Music: 27 Days Later I Have a First Draft,'" *The Guardian*, May 7, 2016, theguardian.com/books/2016/may/07/my-writing-day-ian-rankin.
81 "The slightest interruption": The Wharton information comes primarily from a Mason Currey essay, adapted from his book *Daily Rituals: Women at Work*. Mason Currey, "Famous Women Authors Share Their Daily Writing Routines," Electric Lit, March 15, 2019, electricliterature.com/famous-women-authors-share-their-daily-writing-routines.
82 In it, I recommended: For more on time blocking, see the explanatory video here: timeblockplanner.com.

- 85 **It opened on the story:** Cal Newport, "The Rise and Fall of Getting Things Done," *New Yorker*, November 17, 2020, newyorker.com/tech/annals-of-technology/the-rise-and-fall-of-getting-things-done.
- 89 **docket-clearing meetings:** The careful reader might notice the homage in this name to the delightful *Judge John Hodgman* podcast.
- 90 **"Imagine everyone on your team":** Cal Newport, "It's Time to Embrace Slow Productivity," *New Yorker*, January 3, 2022, newyorker.com/culture/office-space/its-time-to-embrace-slow-productivity.
- 95 **"squeezing everything I could":** Blake, *Free Time*, 4.
- 97 **"I have baked Valentine's cupcakes":** Brigid Schulte, *Overwhelmed: How to Work, Love, and Play When No One Has the Time* (New York: Picador, 2014), 5.
- 98 **she wants to be a teacher:** Schulte, *Overwhelmed*, 13.
- 100 **"Breaking Logjams in Knowledge Work":** Sheila Dodge, Don Kieffer, and Nelson P. Repenning, "Breaking Logjams in Knowledge Work," *MIT Sloan Management Review*, September 6, 2018, https://sloanreview.mit.edu/article/breaking-logjams-in-knowledge-work.

CHAPTER 4: WORK AT A NATURAL PACE

- 112 **It then took another three:** John Gribbin, *The Scientists: A History of Science Told through the Lives of Its Greatest Inventors* (New York: Random House Trade Paperbacks, 2004), 8–9.
- 112 **His classic observations:** Gribbin, *The Scientists*, 45–46.
- 112 **But he didn't get around:** Gribbin, *The Scientists*, 75.
- 113 **"climbed hills, visited grottoes":** Eve Curie, *Madame Curie: A Biography*, transl. Vincent Sheean (New York: Da Capo Press, 2001), 160–62.
- 113 **In this piece, I observed:** Cal Newport, "On Pace and Productivity," *Cal Newport* (blog), July 21, 2021, calnewport.com/blog/2021/07/21/on-pace-and-productivity.
- 115 **"Galileo had a full":** Gribbin, *The Scientists*, 81.
- 117 **"a marginal environment":** Richard B. Lee, "What Hunters Do for a Living, or, How to Make Out on Scarce Resources," in *Man the Hunter*, ed. Richard B. Lee and Irven DeVore (Chicago: Aldine Publishing, 1968), 30.
- 118 **Humans in more or less:** It is impossible to identify a single date on which "modern" *Homo sapiens* arrived. The three-hundred-thousand-year figure is often cited for two reasons. The oldest known *Homo sapiens* fossils, found at the Jebel Irhoud site in Morocco, date roughly to this era (though the fossils include some notably archaic features). Numerous other digs have revealed a widespread transformation of African material culture toward more refined tools around this period as well, as would be expected from the arrival of a species with notably enhanced cognitive capabilities. For a great summary of this data, see Brian Handwerk, "An Evolutionary Timeline of Homo Sapiens," *Smithsonian*, February 2, 2021, smithsonianmag.com/science-nature/essential-timeline-understanding-evolution-homo-sapiens-180976807.

120 **"The Dobe-area Bushmen live":** Lee, "What Hunters Do for a Living," 43.
120 **His big idea, however:** For a more detailed discussion of criticisms and interpretations of Richard Lee's pioneering study, see my November 2022 *New Yorker* article on which much of this section (including all the details and quotes involving Richard Lee and Mark Dyble) is based: Cal Newport, "What Hunter-Gatherers Can Teach Us about the Frustrations of Modern Work," *New Yorker*, November 2, 2022, newyorker.com/culture/office-space/lessons-from-the-deep-history-of-work.
120 **As reported in a landmark:** Mark Dyble, Jack Thorley, Abigail E. Page, Daniel Smith, and Andrea Bamberg Migliano, "Engagement in Agricultural Work Is Associated with Reduced Leisure Time among Agta Hunter-Gatherers," *Nature Human Behaviour* 3, no. 8 (August 2019): 792–96, nature.com/articles/s41562-019-0614-6.
125 **As Rebecca Mead notes:** Rebecca Mead, "All about the Hamiltons," *New Yorker*, February 2, 2015, newyorker.com/magazine/2015/02/09/hamiltons.
126 **"Trying to make musical theater":** Lin-Manuel Miranda, interview by Marc Maron, "Lin-Manuel Miranda," November 14, 2016, in *WTF with Marc Maron*, podcast, 1:37:33, wtfpod.com/podcast/episode-759-lin-manuel-miranda.
126 **"mix of Latin music":** Mead, "All about the Hamiltons."
126 **began staging readings:** Details about the development of *In the Heights* draw from these two useful articles: Susan Dunne, "'In the Heights,' Drafted When Lin-Manuel Miranda Was a Student at Wesleyan University, Opens in Movie Theaters," *Hartford Courant*, June 10, 2021, courant.com/news/connecticut/hc-news-connecticut-wesleyan-in-the-heights-20210610-elvljdtnd5bunegtkuz v3aql2y-story.html; and "How the Eugene O'Neill Theater Center Gave Birth to *In the Heights*," *Playbill*, November 24, 2016, playbill.com/article/how-the-eugene-oneill-theater-center-gave-birth-to-in-the-heights.
136 **chair of the art department:** Norma J. Roberts, ed., *The American Collections: Columbus Museum of Art* (Columbus, OH: Columbus Museum of Art, 1988), 76, archive.org/details/americancollecti0000colu/page/76/mode/2up.
137 **"The lake is perhaps":** Alfred Stieglitz to Sherwood Anderson, August 7, 1924, Alfred Stieglitz/Georgia O'Keeffe Archive, Yale Collection of American Literature, Beinecke Rare Book and Manuscript Library, Yale University, box 2, folder 29, quoted in "Lake George," Alfred Stieglitz Collection, Art Institute of Chicago, archive.artic.edu/stieglitz/lake-george.
138 **working out of her:** Information on O'Keeffe's time at Lake George, including the claim that this was the most prolific period of her career, is from "Georgia O'Keeffe's Lake George Connection," lakegeorge.com, lakegeorge.com/history/georgia-okeeffe. For additional details about the Lake George period, including the specifics of the timing on moving from the mansion to the farmhouse, the name of O'Keeffe's studio, and her morning routine, see Molly Walsh, "O'Keeffe's Footsteps in Lake George Are Nearly Erased," *Seven Days*, June 24, 2015, sevendaysvt.com/vermont/okeeffes-footsteps-in-lake-george-are-nearly-erased/Content?oid=2684054.

139 **It started with a TikTok:** He later changed his username to @ZaidLeppelin.
140 **In early August:** James Tapper, "Quiet Quitting: Why Doing the Bare Minimum at Work Has Gone Global," *The Guardian*, August 6, 2022, theguardian.com/money/2022/aug/06/quiet-quitting-why-doing-the-bare-minimum-at-work-has-gone-global.
140 *The New York Times* **and:** Alyson Krueger, "Who Is Quiet Quitting For?," *New York Times*, August 23, 2022, nytimes.com/2022/08/23/style/quiet-quitting-tiktok.html.
140 **NPR followed with:** Amina Kilpatrick, "What Is 'Quiet Quitting,' and How It May Be a Misnomer for Setting Boundaries at Work," NPR, August 19, 2022, npr.org/2022/08/19/1117753535/quiet-quitting-work-tiktok.
140 **a "really bad idea":** Goh Chiew Tong, "Is 'Quiet Quitting' a Good Idea? Here's What Workplace Experts Say," NPR, August 30, 2022, cnbc.com/2022/08/30/is-quiet-quitting-a-good-idea-heres-what-workplace-experts-say.html.
141 **The old-school Far Left:** For the reader interested in this topic, in December 2022 I published an essay for *The New Yorker* that offered more detailed deconstruction of quiet quitting, including my interpretation of its meaning and importance: Cal Newport, "The Year in Quiet Quitting," *New Yorker*, December 29, 2022, newyorker.com/culture/2022-in-review/the-year-in-quiet-quitting.
143 **"The windows that look":** For details on Ian Fleming and Goldeneye, see: Matthew Parker, *Goldeneye* (New York: Pegasus Books, 2015). Patrick Leigh Fermor's description of the estate has been cited often; see, for example, goldeneye.com/the-story-of-goldeneye, and Robin Hanbury Tenison, "The Friendly Isles: In the Footsteps of Patrick Leigh Fermor," patrickleighfermor.org/2010/04/20/the-friendly-isles-in-the-footsteps-of-patrick-leigh-fermor-by-robin-hanbury-tenison.
146 **"A lot of those days":** Cal Newport, *So Good They Can't Ignore You* (New York: Grand Central, 2012), 126.
150 **"It's sometimes tempting":** "How We Work," in *37signals Employee Handbook*, chap. 9, basecamp.com/handbook/09-how-we-work.
152 **During his** *Steve Allen* **appearance:** A clip of this 1959 interview is available online: Jack Kerouac, interview by Steve Allen, "JACK KEROUAC on THE STEVE ALLEN SHOW with Steve Allen 1959," Historic Films Stock Footage Archive, posted January 12, 2015, YouTube, 6:51, youtube.com/watch?v=3LLpNKo09Xk.
152 **"So he just rolled":** *All Things Considered*, "Jack Kerouac's Famous Scroll, 'On the Road' Again," hosted by Melissa Block and Robert Siegel, aired July 5, 2007 on NPR, npr.org/transcripts/11709924.
153 **"Kerouac cultivated this myth":** "Jack Kerouac's Famous Scroll."
153 **"I think it saved":** Mary Oliver, interview by Krista Tippett, "I Got Saved by the Beauty of the World," February 5, 2015, in *On Being*, podcast, NPR, 49:42, onbeing.org/programs/mary-oliver-i-got-saved-by-the-beauty-of-the-world.
155 **"Inhabited space transcends":** Here is a good summary and discussion of *The Poetics of Space*, which is also my source for the "inhabited space" quote: Tulika

Bahadur, "*The Poetics of Space*," On Art and Aesthetics, October 5, 2016, onartandaesthetics.com/2016/10/05/the-poetics-of-space.

156 **"I love that we are":** Mead, "All about the Hamiltons."
156 **A picture of Gaiman's space:** "Neil Gaiman's Writing Shed," Well-Appointed Desk, July 8, 2014, wellappointeddesk.com/2014/07/neil-gaimans-writing-shed.
156 **Dan Brown, for his part:** Sarah Lyall, "The World according to Dan Brown," *New York Times*, September 30, 2017, nytimes.com/2017/09/30/books/dan-brown-origin.html.
157 **Francis Ford Coppola has:** Francis Ford Coppola, director's commentary, *The Conversation*, special ed. DVD, directed by Francis Ford Coppola (Hollywood, CA: Paramount Pictures, 2000).
158 **As John McPhee revealed:** John McPhee, "Tabula Rasa: Volume Two," *New Yorker*, April 12, 2021, newyorker.com/magazine/2021/04/19/tabula-rasa-volume-two.
159 **I originally told these:** Many of the stories and all of the quotes in this section come from my original article on this topic: Cal Newport, "What If Remote Work Didn't Mean Working from Home?," *New Yorker*, May 21, 2021, newyorker.com/culture/cultural-comment/remote-work-not-from-home.
160 **Mystery rituals developed in the sixth century BCE:** Karen Armstrong, *The Case for God* (New York and Toronto: Knopf, 2009), 54.
161 **initiates from the previous year's ritual:** Armstrong, *Case for God*, 56.
162 **"summary of the religious process":** Armstrong, *Case for God*, 56.
163 **David Lynch would order:** Mason Currey, *Daily Rituals: How Artists Work* (New York: Knopf, 2013), 121.
163 **N. C. Wyeth would wake:** Currey, *Daily Rituals*, 177.
163 **Anne Rice wrote *Interview with the Vampire*:** Currey, *Daily Rituals*, 216.
163 **Gertrude Stein would wake:** Currey, *Daily Rituals*, 49–50.

CHAPTER 5: OBSESS OVER QUALITY

166 **Jewel started joining her parents:** It's interesting to note that Jewel was not the only female singing sensation of the 1990s to live through this same experience of performing long shows at bars with her parents at an inappropriately young age. As revealed in the 2022 documentary *Shania Twain: Not Just a Girl*, Shania Twain also learned her craft as a young child, crooning in bars with her mom. According to the documentary, Twain would sometimes be forced to stay up for the after-hours shows, taking place after the bar was officially closed, as a means of circumventing the law that said she was too young to be in a drinking establishment during business hours.
166 **"honky-tonks, juke joints":** Jewel, *Never Broken: Songs Are Only Half the Story* (New York: Blue Rider Press, 2016), 21.
168 **"Do you think you can":** Jewel, interview by Joe Rogan, "Jewel Turned Down $1 Million Record Deal When She Was Homeless," October 25, 2021, in *The*

Joe Rogan Experience, podcast, 3:06, youtube.com/watch?v=DTGtC7FC4oI (hereafter referred to as *JRE* 1724).

168 "bleeding my heart out": *JRE* 1724, 5:25.
169 "Every label came down": *JRE* 1724, 9:30.
169 "I turned down": *JRE* 1724, 12:38.
170 "I had to put myself": *JRE* 1724, 13:20.
170 "I was just doing it": *JRE* 1724, 14:00.
170 "To not leverage my art": See interviews with Jewel, for example: Taylor Dunn, "Why Jewel Says She Turned Down a Million-Dollar Signing Bonus When She Was Homeless," ABC News, abcnews.go.com/Business/jewel-talks-human-growing-career-slowly/story?id=46598431.
171 "Radio hated me": Jewel, interview by Hrishikesh Hirway, "Jewel—You Were Meant for ME," episode 198, *Song Exploder*, podcast, 17:58, transcript available at songexploder.net/transcripts/jewel-transcript.pdf.
171 This allowed Jewel to focus: Jewel, *Never Broken*, 173.
171 At one point, she even: Jewel, *Never Broken*, 177.
172 He gave her a critical: Jewel, *Never Broken*, 230.
172 "It was staggering": Jewel, *Never Broken*, 231.
176 "Which ones do I tell": Jason Fell, "How Steve Jobs Saved Apple," NBC News, October 30, 2011, nbcnews.com/id/wbna45095399.
176 "Deciding what not to do": Jason Fell, "How Steve Jobs Saved Apple," *Entrepreneur*, October 27, 2011, entrepreneur.com/growing-a-business/how-steve-jobs-saved-apple/220604.
178 "I just wasn't sure": Jewel, *Never Broken*, 270.
180 "glass cube in the sky": Paul Jarvis, "Working Remotely on an Island: A Day in the Life of a Company of One," Penguin UK, penguin.co.uk/articles/2019/04/working-remotely-on-an-island-company-of-one-paul-jarvis.
180 "My wife and I had": Cameron McCool, "Entrepreneur on the Island: A Conversation with Paul Jarvis," *Bench* (blog), June 3, 2016, bench.co/blog/small-business-stories/paul-jarvis.
180 "When you're remote": McCool, "Entrepreneur on the Island."
181 "I typically rise": Jarvis, "Working Remotely on an Island."
183 "But it's like there's": Ira Glass, "Ira Glass on Storytelling 3," posted July 11, 2009, warphotography, YouTube, 5:20, youtube.com/watch?v=X2wLP0izeJE.
183 "You find yourself back": Anne Lamott, *Bird by Bird: Some Instructions on Writing and Life* (New York: Anchor, 1994; rpt. 2019), 8.
184 I can see brilliance: For more on this shot, see V. Renée, "Here's What the First 3 Minutes of 'Boogie Nights' Can Teach You about Shot Economy," No Film School, September 26, 2016, nofilmschool.com/2016/09/heres-what-first-3-minutes-boogie-nights-can-teach-you-about-shot-economy.
185 "I remember when I finished": Ira Glass, interview by Michael Lewis, "Other People's Money: Ira Glass on Finding Your Voice," March 1, 2022, in *Against the Rules*, podcast, 26:46, pushkin.fm/podcasts/against-the-rules/other-peoples-money-ira-glass-on-finding-your-voice.

185 **Of these five finalists:** The 2021 awards were the most recent to have been given out when I wrote this chapter in 2022. Of the five finalists in 2021, Avni Doshi was the only one without any connection to an MFA program. Indeed, the fact that she didn't attend such a program is considered unusual enough that it's mentioned in interviews; for example, see Sana Goyal, "'The Shape of This Moment': In Conversation with Avni Doshi," *The Margins*, Asian American Writers' Workshop, April 21, 2021, aaww.org/the-shape-of-this-moment-in-conversation-with-avni-doshi.

187 **Did you know, for example:** Vashi Nedomansky, "The Editing of MAD MAX: Fury Road," VashiVisuals, May 30, 2015, vashivisuals.com/the-editing-of-mad-max-fury-road.

190 **Indeed, Tolkien biographer:** Raymond Edwards, *Tolkien* (Ramsbury, UK: Robert Hale, 2020), 165–67.

190 **"The Inklings was, above all else":** Edwards, *Tolkien*.

191 **Alexander Graham Bell's carefully maintained:** See, for example, the following article about the dispute that contains some nice images of Graham's notebook: Seth Shulman, "The Telephone Gambit: Chasing Alexander Graham Bell's Secret," *Patently-O* (blog), January 10, 2008, patentlyo.com/patent/2008/01/the-telephone-g.html.

194 **created a "major backlash":** Clifford Williamson, "1966: The Beatles' Tumultuous World Tour," History Extra, June 1, 2017, historyextra.com/period/20th-century/1966-the-beatles-tumultuous-world-tour.

195 **more than thirty-five thousand police:** Mark Lewisohn, *The Complete Beatles Chronicle: The Definitive Day-by-Day Guide to the Beatles' Entire Career* (Chicago: Chicago Review Press, 1992; rpt. 2010), 211.

195 **The next tour stop:** Williamson, "1966: The Beatles' Tumultuous World Tour."

195 **it was "a summons":** Williamson, "1966: The Beatles' Tumultuous World Tour."

195 **"more popular than Jesus":** Williamson, "1966: The Beatles' Tumultuous World Tour." For more on the 1966 *Evening Standard* crisis, see Lewisohn, *The Complete Beatles Chronicle*.

196 **"With the producer George Martin":** Jon Pareles, "Pop View; At Age 20, Sgt. Pepper Marches On," *New York Times*, May 31, 1987, nytimes.com/1987/05/31/arts/pop-view-at-age-20-sgt-pepper-marches-on.html.

197 **"critics vilify 'Sgt. Pepper'":** Pareles, "Pop View; At Age 20, Sgt. Pepper Marches On."

199 **While still a child:** Morgan Greenwald, "19 Celebrities Who Got Their Start on 'Star Search,'" *Best Life*, September 16, 2020, bestlifeonline.com/star-search-celebrities.

199 **Her perky stage presence:** Details on Alanis Morissette's early career come from *Jagged*, directed by Alison Klayman (HBO Documentary Films, 2021).

200 **With the help of her:** Jean-Francois Méan, "Interview with Scott Welch, Manager for Alanis Morissette," *HitQuarters*, August 6, 2002, web.archive.org/web/20120609212424/http://www.hitquarters.com/index.php3?page=intrview%2Fopar%2Fintrview_SWelch.html.

200 "She just wanted to be an *artist*": Lyndsey Parker, "Glen Ballard Recalls Making Alanis Morissette's 'Jagged Little Pill,' 25 Years Later: 'I Was Just Hoping That Someone Would Hear It,'" *Yahoo!Entertainment*, September 25, 2020, yahoo.com/entertainment/glen-ballard-recalls-making-alanis-morissettes-jagged-little-pill-25-years-later-i-was-just-hoping-that-someone-would-hear-it-233222384.html.

203 "From that point on, not": "The Story of Twilight and Getting Published," Stephenie Meyer, stepheniemeyer.com/the-story-of-twilight-getting-published, accessed December 2022.

203 This left Cussler: Michael Carlson, "Clive Cussler Obituary," *The Guardian*, February 27, 2020, theguardian.com/books/2020/feb/27/clive-cussler-obituary.

204 "Anyone who wanted to look": John Noble Wilford, "For Michael Crichton, Medicine Is for Writing," *New York Times*, June 15, 1970, nytimes.com/1970/06/15/archives/for-michael-crichton-medicine-is-for-writing.html.

204 He began crafting his first: Nicholas Wroe, "A Life in Writing: John Grisham," *The Guardian*, November 25, 2011, theguardian.com/culture/2011/nov/25/john-grisham-life-in-writing.

207 It was at this point: Carlson, "Clive Cussler Obituary."

207 Grisham didn't stop practicing: Movie rights bid from the *Los Angeles Times*, July 17, 1993, latimes.com/archives/la-xpm-1993-07-17-mn-14067-story.html.

209 "It grabs hold of the audience": "Assault on Precinct 13," BAMPFA, bampfa.org/event/assault-precinct-13.

209 It was there in London: "Behind the Scenes: Halloween," Wayback Machine Internet Archive, web.archive.org/web/20061220013740/http://halloweenmovies.com/filmarchive/h1bts.htm.

209 "We basically shamed Moustapha": "Behind the Scenes: Halloween."

210 The film went on: "Halloween," Box Office Mojo, IMDbPro, boxofficemojo.com/release/rl1342342657, accessed December 2022.

CONCLUSION

213 "The note-typing could take": John McPhee, *Draft No. 4: On the Writing Process* (New York: Farrar, Straus and Giroux, 2018), 35.

214 A standard long-form: McPhee, *Draft No. 4*, 37.

214 *Encounters with the Archdruid*, McPhee's: McPhee, *Draft No. 4*, 25.

214 McPhee would photocopy: McPhee, *Draft No. 4*, 35–37.

214 "an essential part of my": McPhee, *Draft No. 4*, 21.

215 "The procedure eliminated nearly all": McPhee, *Draft No. 4*, 35–36.

218 "And if somebody says": John McPhee, interview by Peter Hessler, "John McPhee, the Art of Nonfiction No. 3," *Paris Review*, Spring 2010, theparisreview.org/interviews/5997/the-art-of-nonfiction-no-3-john-mcphee.

INDEX

academia, 16, 19, 24–25, 70, 76, 129, 138, 175, 205, 216
   administrative tasks, 65, 72
   back-and-forth messaging for, 56, 87–89
   contain with autopilot, 83–85
   hire managers/services for, 95–96, 99
   limit them/tame them, 78–83, 133
   and limiting daily goals, 75
   make others work on, 90–93
   pick projects with fewer ones, 93–94, 99
   reverse task list and, 91
   simplify with software, 95–96
   synchronize them, 85–89
   task engines and, 93–94
   See also overhead tax
agriculture, 16–18, 117–24, 139
Agta community, 120–22, 124
Akkad, Moustapha, 209–11
Alanis (Morissette album), 199–200
Allen, David, 85–88
Allen, Steve, 151–53
ambition, 42–43, 75–76, 103, 115, 131–32, 169, 183
Angelou, Maya, 40, 158, 160
anthropology studies, 117–22
anti-productivity movement, 3–6, 99, 217
Apple, 36–37, 57, 176
Aristotle, 115, 162

Armstrong, Karen, 160–62
artists, 39–42, 136–39, 142, 145, 163, 206, 208. *See also specific names*
Assault on Precinct 13 (film), 209–10
assembly-line work, 17–20, 100–101, 124
Atlantic Records, 170–71, 174
@ZKChillen video, 139–40
Austen, Jane, 42, 47–54, 60, 65
Austen-Leigh, James Edward, 48–49, 52
autonomy, 20, 43, 49, 123, 125, 216. *See also* freelancers; solopreneurs

Bachelard, Gaston, 154–55
Ballard, Glen, 200–201
Basecamp, 150–51
Beatles, 194–98
Benchley, Peter, 40, 157–58, 160
Benchley, Wendy, 157–58
Bird by Bird (Lamott), 183–84
Blake, Jenny, 71, 75, 95, 145–46
Bloomberg, 55
Brahe, Tycho, 112
brain, the, 39, 60, 63, 118, 159
Brands, H. W., 77–79
"Breaking Logjams in Knowledge Work," 100–104
Broad Institute, 100–104
Brower, David, 214
Brown, Dan, 156–57

Brown, Fred, 2–3
Bruckheimer, Jerry, 27
Burkeman, Oliver, 4
burnout
   alternatives to, 38, 42, 77–78, 215
   knowledge work and, 124, 215
   and overhead tax, 61–63
   technology and, 23–25
busyness, 21, 88
   alternatives to, 7–9, 29, 35–36, 49, 53
   balance with rest projects, 149–51
   Benjamin Franklin and, 76–77
   and focusing on quality, 173, 176
   leads to exhaustion, 5–6, 115
   and limiting projects, 73–75
   modern bias towards, 6, 53–54, 116
   periods of, 29, 134–35, 138–39, 147–53, 151–53, 171, 205
   stepping back from, 115, 177, 219
   visible activity and, 22–25

calls, limiting of, 133–34, 141, 147–48, 177
Candlestick Park (San Francisco), 194, 196
Can't Even (Petersen), 4
capitalists, 17–20
Carpenter, John, 209–11
Carter, Bill, 13, 26–27
Case for God, The (Armstrong), 160–62
Casino Royale (Fleming), 144
CBS, 13, 22–23, 25–29
Challenger disaster, 73
Charteris, Ann, 144
Cinema Speculation (Tarantino), 187
cognitive work, 18, 38–39, 62, 83, 124, 132–33, 217
collaboration, 19, 56–58, 87–89, 142
Company of One (Jarvis), 179
computers, 62, 214
   and burnout crisis, 23–25
   innovations in, 23, 87, 176, 202
   programmers of, 38, 193
   pseudo-productivity and, 23–25
   science of, 70, 76, 130, 180, 191–92

containment, notion of, 83
conversations, real-time, 88–89
Cook, Tim, 36–37
Copernicus, 111–13, 115
Coppola, Francis Ford, 149, 157
coronavirus pandemic
   and anti-productivity movement, 3–6, 99
   more meetings/video calls in, 55–58
   quiet quitting and, 140
   and shift to telecommuting, 57–58
   and workplace changes, 3–6, 36–38, 99, 159, 217
creative work, 3, 9, 52, 86
   and attracting an investor, 209–11
   eccentric spaces for, 40, 157–60
   and freedom to experiment, 196–99
   limit your missions for, 70
   and obsessing over quality, 196–99
   seasonal approach to, 137–39
   seasonal escapes for, 144–45
   sparked by rituals, 162–63
   and taste/ability, 182–86, 188, 190–91, 199
   unfolds slowly, 128–29
Crichton, Michael, 203–4, 207
CSI, 27–29
Cundey, Dean, 210
Curie, Marie, 113–14, 125, 138
Currey, Mason, 48, 163
Cussler, Clive, 203, 206–8

Da Vinci Code (Brown), 156–57
Daily Rituals (Currey), 48, 163
Datebook, 196
Davenport, Tom, 16, 19–20
deep work, 21, 25, 40, 64, 68, 82, 115, 177
Deep Work, 72–73, 82
Desperate Networks (Carter), 13, 26–27
DeVore, Irven, 119
Digital Minimalism, 186
distractions, 23, 52, 67, 78–83, 147–48, 215

Do Fewer Things
    advantages of, 59–60, 63–65, 99–100
    "contain the small," 76–85, 95–96, 106
    examples of, 47–54, 63–65
    as first principle, 8, 41, 53–54, 60, 216
    focus on less, 59–60, 64–71, 75–76
    and hire managers/services, 95–96
    invest money in, 95–96, 99
    limit missions/daily goals/projects, 69–76
    "limit the big," 66–69
    and make others work more, 90–93
    and obsessing over quality, 173–74, 177
    organizational strategies for, 83–89
    pull-based workflow and, 100–105
    the reasons to do it, 54–59, 177
Do Nothing (Headlee), 4–5
Draft No. 4 (McPhee), 1, 213, 217
Drucker, Peter, 15, 20, 218
Dyble, Mark, 120–22

Ebert, Roger, 187
economic growth, 16–18
educators, 138. *See also* professors; teachers
Edwards, Raymond, 190
Effective Executive, The (Drucker), 20
efficiency, 17–19, 31, 61, 78, 94, 99
Eleusinian Mysteries, 161–62
emails, 7, 21, 66
    high quantity of, 55
    limit them/tame them, 75, 82, 141, 182
    and office collaboration, 87–89
    an overhead tax, 56, 59
    protocols for, 84, 177
    as visible activity, 23
EMI Studios (London), 196–98
Encounters with the Archdruid (McPhee), 214
Entfremdung (Marx), 123
entrepreneurs, 20–21, 61, 95–96, 145, 206–9
Epstein, Brian, 195

exhaustion
    anti-productivity movement and, 4–6
    and being overloaded, 60, 135
    how to combat it, 7–9, 71, 124, 149
    and overhead tax, 63
    reasons for, 5–6, 18, 22–25, 55, 115

Fair Labor Standards Act, 37, 98, 123
farming, 16–18, 117–24, 139
fast food, 31–34, 37–38
Fathom Analytics, 181
Fermat, Pierre de, 66–68, 70
Fermat's Enigma (Singh), 66
Feynman, Richard, 72–73
films/film industry, 184, 186–89, 207, 209–11. *See also specific film titles*
Firm, The (Grisham), 204, 206–7
Fleming, Ian, 142–46, 203
Ford, Henry, 18–19
Ford Motor Company, 18–19
43 Folders blog, 86
Four Thousand Weeks (Burkeman), 4
Franklin, Benjamin, 42, 76–80, 82–83
Franklin, Jane, 82
Free Time (Blake), 71, 95
freelancers, 20–21, 43, 61, 84–85, 130, 146, 180–81, 216
Fried, Jason, 150
Frostick, Jonathan, 54–57, 61

Gaiman, Neil, 156
Galileo, 42, 112, 114–16
Gates, Bill, 202
genetic sequencing pipeline, 100–104
Getting Things Done (GTD) method, 85–88
Gibson, Debbie, 199–200
Glass, Ira, 182–86
Graham, William, 73
Great Movies, The (Ebert), 187
Great Resignation, 4–5
Greece, ancient, 160–62
Gribbin, John, 111–12, 114–15

Grisham, John, 204, 206–7
Guardian, The, 140

Hall, David, 78–79, 81
Halloween (film), 210
Hamilton (musical), 134–35, 156
"Hand in My Pocket" (Morissette song), 201
Harrison, George, 195–97
Harter, Jim, 24
Harvard, 202–4
Headlee, Celeste, 4–5
Hemingway, Ernest, 70, 185
historic thinkers, 111–16, 163, 191
Honoré, Carl, 35
Horizon (BBC show), 72–73
hourly wage service sector, 62
Hudes, Quiara Alegría, 127
hunter-gatherers, 117–24, 132, 139

In Praise of Slowness (Honoré), 35
In the Heights (musical), 125–29, 131
income, 140
  sacrificed for quality, 145–47, 205–8
  traded for freedom, 175–76, 179–82
  traded for time, 64, 71, 78–80, 145
  turning it down, 169–70, 175–76, 201
industrial labor, 17–22, 25, 62, 97–98, 114, 122–24, 139
Industrial Revolution, 17–18, 122–24
Inklings, the, 189–90
Inner Change Coffeehouse (San Diego), 165–66, 168–70
insight, moments of, 2–3, 29, 42, 111
Interlochen Arts Academy, 167
Interview with the Vampire (Rice), 163
It Doesn't Have to Be Crazy at Work (Fried), 150
Italy, 31–35, 114

Jagged Little Pill (Morissette album), 199–201
James Bond spy thrillers, 142–46, 203
Jane Austen: A Life (Tomalin), 50–52

Japan, 194–95
Jarvis, Paul, 178–82
Jaws (Benchley), 157–58
Jewel, 165–78, 181, 199, 201
Jobs, Steve, 176
journalism, long-form, 1–3, 213–16
Ju/'hoansi community, 117–20

Kail, Thomas, 126–27
Keith, Ben, 170–72
Kemsley Newspapers, 142–43
Kerouac, Jack, 151–53
Kickstarter, 37
knowledge work
  core activities of, 174–75, 181–82
  discontentment with, 3–7, 9, 217
  emergence of, 18–21, 114, 123–24, 217
  flexibility of, 139, 180
  general definition of, 38–39
  during the pandemic, 3–6
  self-regulation of, 62–63
  traditional, 7, 38–40, 42–43
"Knowledge-Worker Productivity: The Biggest Challenge" (Drucker), 15

labor unions, 98, 123–24
Lake George, New York, 137–39, 142, 145, 147
Lamott, Anne, 183–84
Laziness Does Not Exist (Price), 4
Lean In, 23–24
Lee, Richard, 117–21
legislation, 37, 98, 123–24, 218
leisure time
  balance with intense effort, 134–35, 149–50
  dedicate to projects, 202–5, 208
  importance of, 186–87
  of prehistoric peoples, 119, 121–22
  reset your mind with, 148–49
  See also retreats/vacations
Lennon, John, 195–96
Lewis, C. S., 189–90

Lewis, Michael, 184–85
Lincolnshire, England, 112, 114, 138
LinkedIn, 54
Little, Brown and Company, 205
London, England, 40, 47, 78–79, 144, 196, 209
Lord of the Rings, The (Tolkien), 190
Los Angeles, 200–201
Los Angeles Times, 73
Lowe's, 37
Lynch, David, 163

Mad Max: Fury Road (film), 187
"Man the Hunter" (conference), 119
Manhattan Times, 128
Mann, Merlin, 85–87, 89
manufacturing, 17–22, 62, 101, 139
Marcos, Imelda and Ferdinand, 195
market economy, 218
market value, 38
Martin, George, 196
Marx, Karl, 123
mathematicians, 66–69
Maverick Records, 201
MCA, 199–200
McCartney, Paul, 196, 198
McCullough, David, 158, 160
McDonald's, 31–33, 37
McKinsey, 23–24
McPhee, John, 1–3, 6–7, 29, 39–40, 158, 213–19
Mead, Rebecca, 125–26, 134–35
meaningful work, 29, 52, 71, 96, 136, 148, 160, 174, 219. *See also* deep work; projects: advance meaningful ones
Mediterranean Caper, The (Cussler), 206–7
meetings, 7, 59, 75
 autopilot schedule and, 85
 ban for one day a week, 147–48
 docket-clearing, 89
 limit them/tame them, 133–34, 177, 182

 pull-based workflow and, 103
 and simulated slow seasons, 142
 synchronize them, 57, 88–89
 virtual, 36, 55–58
 See also Zoom; Zoom Apocalypse
mental space, 52, 96, 148, 160
mental state, 162–63
Meyer, Stephenie, 202–3, 205
MFA programs, 185–86
Microsoft, 55, 181, 202
Miller, George, 187
Miranda, Lin-Manuel, 42, 125–29, 131, 134–35, 156
missions (professional), 69–76
MIT, 100, 130, 191
MIT Sloan Management Review, 100–104
Moonves, Leslie, 13, 22–23, 25–29
Morris-Jumel Mansion (New York), 156
Morissette, Alanis, 199–201
Mount, the (Berkshires), 81
musical theater, 125–29, 131, 134–35, 156
music/musicians, 194–202
Mystery cults/rituals, 160–62

National Science Foundation, 192
natural world, 153–56, 160, 162, 179, 181–82
Nature Human Behaviour, 120
Neolithic era, 161
Neolithic Revolution, 122
New York City, 77, 125–29, 135–38, 140, 156
New York Times, The, 140, 196, 203
New Yorker, The, 1–7, 37, 85, 90–93, 125–26, 158, 217
Newton, Isaac, 40, 43, 112–14, 138
Nicomachean Ethics (Aristotle), 115
novelists, 40, 47, 80, 129, 142, 151, 156–57, 183–86, 192, 202–8. *See also specific names*
Now Is the Time (Morissette album), 200
NPR, 140, 153–54, 182–83

obligations, 19, 48–54, 63, 67–71, 82, 86–90, 93
Obsess Over Quality
   announce a schedule, 208–9
   and attracting an investor, 209–11
   bet on yourself, 199–211
   of core activities, 174–75
   definition of, 173–74
   and do fewer things, 59–60, 63–65, 173–74, 177
   examples of, 165–73, 178–82
   immerse in other fields, 186–89
   improve your taste, 182–91, 199
   and like-minded people, 189–91
   pseudo-productivity and, 24–25, 182
   reasons to do it, 174–82
   and risk of perfectionism, 193–99
   and risk-taking, 199–201
   by simplifying, 176–77, 182
   and slower pace, 170–82, 197–99, 201
   spare time strategy for, 202–5
   and taking time off, 150
   as third principle, 8, 41, 216
   tools for, 191–93
   turn down income for, 169–70, 175–76, 201, 205–8
office managers, 14, 92, 217
O'Keeffe, Georgia, 42, 136–39, 142
O'Leary, Kevin, 140
Oliver, Mary, 42, 153–56, 160, 162
"On Pace and Productivity," 113
On the Revolutions of the Celestial Spheres (Copernicus), 112
On the Road (Kerouac), 151–53
operations managers, 95–96
organizational strategies
   autopilot schedule, 83–85
   double project timelines, 131–32
   engineered simplicity, 54
   Getting Things Done (GTD), 85–88
   pseudo-productivity, 23
   pull-based workflow, 100–110
   slow productivity, 40–41
   See also time: blocking of

Out of the Silent Planet (Lewis), 189
overhead tax, 56–63, 83, 106. *See also* administrative tasks
Overwhelmed: How to Work, Love, and Play When No One Has the Time (Schulte), 97–98
Oxford University, 68, 189

pace, accelerated, 33, 35. *See also* busyness
pace, natural/humane. *See* Work at a Natural Pace
Paramount (film studio), 207
Pareles, Jon, 196–98
parents, 4, 97–99, 203
Paris Review, The, 218–19
Patiño, Juan, 171–72
Pennington, New Jersey, 157–58, 160
perfectionism, 193–99
performative
   measures, 15, 18–20, 217
   rewards, 117
Petersen, Anne Helen, 4
Petrini, Carlo, 31–35, 38, 40, 42
Philippines, 120–22, 194–95
philosophers, 39, 78, 154
physicists, 72–73, 112–14
Pieces of You (Jewel album), 171
playwrights, 39, 127–28. *See also specific names*
Please Please Me (Beatles album), 197
Plimpton, George, 158
podcasts/podcasters, 5, 82, 96, 181, 184, 193
Poetics of Space, The (Bachelard), 154–55
poets/poetry, 115, 151, 153–56, 160
Pollan, Michael, 33–34
prehistoric ancestors. *See* hunter-gatherers
Price, Devon, 4
Princeton University, 1, 7, 66–68
Principia (Newton), 43
productivity
   academic studies on, 15–16
   alternative approaches to, 7–9, 26–29, 33–35

definition of, 7–9, 13–22
metrics of, 16–25
new vision of, 38
notions/concepts of, 3–4, 27–29, 114, 217–18
quantitative approach to, 15, 18, 25
twentieth-century beliefs about, 13–21, 25–29, 217
professional services, 95–96
professors, 43, 57–58, 64, 66–71, 84–85, 186, 192
profits, 18, 62, 77–79, 176
projects
   acknowledgement messages for, 107–8
   advance meaningful ones, 53, 69, 78–83, 96
   and attracting an investor, 209–11
   balance with rest projects, 149–51
   blocking time for, 148–49
   dedicate free time to, 202–5
   double timelines for, 131–32
   limiting them, 72–76, 180
   and periods of intensity, 151–53
   pull-based workflow for, 105–10
   and simulated slow seasons, 141–42
   slowing down for, 39, 114–17
   take breaks between, 146
   taking longer on, 128–29, 132, 135
   tracking them, 74
pseudo-productivity
   alternatives to, 33–35, 175, 216, 219
   bad side effects of, 37–41, 97–99, 124
   deterioration of, 22–23
   explanation of, 21–25, 123–25
   knowledge workers and, 22, 65
   mindset of, 128–29
   and pursuit of quality, 24–25, 182
   self-imposed, 43
   technology and, 23–25, 29
   visible activity and, 20–25, 29, 98–99, 123, 217
pull-based workflow, 100–110
push-based workflow, 101–2, 104–5

quality. *See* Obsess Over Quality
quiet quitting, 4–5, 139–42, 151

Raise the Titanic! (Cussler), 208
Rankin, Ian, 80–81
remote work, 54, 180
   during the pandemic, 5, 36–37, 57–58
   eccentric spaces for, 159–60
   productivity metrics for, 20–21
   pseudo-productivity and, 43
Renaissance, 112–13, 115
Reservoir Dogs (film), 186, 188
retreats/vacations, 113–14, 125, 137–39, 142–47, 204
Revolver (Beatles album), 194
rhythm, of work, 9, 51, 84–85, 114–16, 122–25, 138–39
Ribet, Ken, 67
Rice, Anne, 163
"Rise and Fall of Getting Things Done, The," 85
rituals, 7, 84–85, 122–23, 155, 160–63
Roman Empire, 122
Room of One's Own, A (Woolf), 49
Rubincam, Anna, 40

Salone del Gusto (Turin), 32
Sampas, Jack, 152–53
San Diego, 165–69
Schulte, Brigid, 97–98
scientists, 39–43, 100–102, 111–16, 124, 128, 138, 191–92
Scientists, The (Gribbin), 111–12, 114
screenwriters, 26–27, 192–93, 208. *See also specific names*
seasonality
   embracing it, 136–39
   of prehistoric peoples, 139
   schedule slow seasons, 139–42
   shorter work year and, 142–47
   simulated, 116, 141–42, 145
   "small," 147–51
   and working in cycles, 150–51
self-employed, 142, 146–47

Sgt. Pepper's Lonely Hearts Club Band (Beatles album), 197–98
Shark Tank, 140
simplifying
　advantages of, 63–64
　importance of, 53–54
　and narrowing your focus, 70–71
　and pursuit of quality, 176–77, 182
　of your workload, 66–71
　See also Do Fewer Things
singers/songwriters, 165–78
Singh, Simon, 66–68
Slack, 23–24, 55, 88
Slow Food movement, 31–35
slow productivity
　advantages of, 39, 77–80, 125, 219
　explanation of, 8–9, 41, 215–19
　introduction to, 1–7
　invest money in, 191–93
　key tenets of, 132
　main principles of, 8, 41, 53–54, 60, 216
　mindset of, 128–29
　philosophy of, 40–44
　and traditional knowledge workers, 38–40
　See also Do Fewer Things; Obsess Over Quality; Work at a Natural Pace
slow seasons. *See* seasonality: schedule slow seasons
slowness revolution, 33–35, 38
small-business owners, 9, 20, 43, 61, 71, 180, 216
So Good They Can't Ignore You, 146
social capital, 208–9
software, 19–20
　for administrative tasks, 57, 95–96, 142
　companies of, 23, 150, 181, 202
　for writing, 192–93
　See also Zoom
solopreneurs, 43, 54, 105, 216
Spirit (Jewel album), 178
Starr, Ringo, 196
Stein, Gertrude, 163

Steinbeck, John, 158–59
Steve Allen Show, The, 151–53
Stieglitz, Alfred, 137
stress, 5, 9, 24, 62–63, 84–85, 130, 144, 149, 159, 172
Substack, 145–46
Sullivan, Andrew, 145–46

Takano, Mark, 37
Taniyama-Shimura conjecture, 67–68
Tarantino, Quentin, 186–88
tasks. *See* administrative tasks
Tassler, Nina, 27–29
Taylor, Frederick Winslow, 18–19
teachers, 64, 128, 136
teams, 89–92, 101–5, 150, 175, 177
technology
　and burnout crisis, 23–25
　and office collaboration, 87–89
　and the pandemic, 57–58
　pseudo-productivity and, 23–25, 29, 217
　pull-based workflow and, 102–5
　See also software
telecommuting, 23, 36–37, 57–58
Thinking for a Living: How to Get Better Performance and Results from Knowledge Workers (Davenport), 16
This American Life (radio show), 182–83
"tickler file," 86
TikTok, 139–40
time
　blocking of, 74, 82–84, 133–34, 148–49, 177
　for deep work, 25, 72
　estimates are difficult, 132–33, 135–36
　income traded for, 71, 78–80, 145
　managing it, 73–75, 79, 82–83
　and need to limit projects, 73–75
　pull-based workflow and, 106–7
　reclaiming it, 95–96, 106
Time to Kill, A (Grisham), 204, 206
timelines, 115–17, 131–35, 152

timescales, 8, 29, 113–14, 118, 131–33, 147
Tolkien, J. R. R., 52, 189–90
Tomalin, Claire, 50–52
Trello board, 91
Twilight (Meyer), 202–3

United Kingdom, 37
video conferencing, 55–58, 88
visible activity, 20–25, 29, 53, 98–99, 123, 217

websites
 consultants for, 96
 designers of, 85, 110, 179–81
 launching of, 131–32
 updating of, 19, 72, 85, 107–10
Welch, Scott, 200
Wesleyan University, 125–28, 131
Wharton, Edith, 81
Whitehead, Colson, 185–86
"Who Will Save Your Soul" (Jewel song), 167, 172
Wiles, Andrew, 66–70
Williamson, Clifford, 194–95
Wilson, Brian, 198
Wlaschin, Ken, 209
Woolf, Virginia, 49
Work at a Natural Pace
 advantages of, 43, 60, 76, 116, 142
 ancient examples of, 117–24
 double project timelines, 131–32
 embrace seasonality, 136–39
 explanation of, 29, 115–25
 make five-year plan, 129–31
 modern examples of, 125–29
 no meeting Mondays and, 147–48
 and obsessing over quality, 170–78, 197–98
 rituals for, 160–63
 schedule rest projects, 149–51
 schedule slow seasons, 139–42
 scientists as example of, 111–16, 124, 128

 as second principle, 8–9, 41, 216
 shorter work year and, 142–47
 simplify your workday, 133–35
 Slow Food movement and, 35
 "small seasonality" and, 147–51
 strategies for, 129–36
 and varying work intensity, 147–53
 work in cycles, 150–51
 work poetically, 153–63
 and your surroundings, 153–63
work schedule
 autopilot, 83–85
 control over, 75, 181
 forty-hour weeks, 21, 123
 four-day week, 37
 getting creative with, 202–5
 in-person, 36–37
 no meeting Mondays, 147–48
 and obsessing over quality, 202–8
 one project per day, 75–76
 reducing it, 37–38, 64, 71, 75, 179, 207
 shorter work year and, 142–47
 simplify each day, 133–35
 take off random days, 147
work spaces
 eccentric, 157–60, 163
 home offices, 36, 54, 58, 67, 69, 155–60
 match your space to your work, 155–57
 rituals and, 84–85, 155, 162–63
 task blocks and, 84–85
 working poetically and, 153–57
 See also remote work
work-life balance, 23–24, 41
 and doing fewer things, 64, 97–100
 examples of, 115–17, 145
 and pursuit of quality, 174, 181–82
World Without Email, A, 82
writers
 eccentric spaces for, 157–60, 163
 as knowledge workers, 39
 and quitting day job, 205–8
 and seasonal approach, 138
 shorter work year and, 145–46

writers *(cont.)*
    simplifying workload and, 70
    and slow productivity, 49, 213–19
    software for, 192–93
    spare time strategy for, 202–5
    writers' groups and, 189–91
    See also journalism, long-form; *specific names*
Wyeth, N. C., 163

Yablans, Irwin, 209
"You Were Meant for Me" (Jewel song), 167, 172
Young, Lulu, 146
Young, Neil, 170–72

Zoom, 5, 24, 62–63, 88, 95, 99
Zoom Apocalypse, 55–58, 61
Zuiker, Anthony, 26–29